Dance: A Very Social History

Dance
A Very Social History

by Carol McD. Wallace, Don McDonagh, Jean L. Druesedow,
Laurence Libin, and Constance Old

The Metropolitan Museum of Art, New York
Rizzoli, New York

This book was published on the occasion of an exhibition held at the Costume
Institute of The Metropolitan Museum of Art, New York, from December 17,
1986 through September 6, 1987. This exhibition has been made possible by
Shiseido Cosmetics.

John P. O'Neill, *Editor in Chief*
Barbara Burn, *Project Supervisor*
Andrew Solomon, *Picture Researcher*
Roberta Savage, *Designer*

Type set by Concept Typographic Services, New York
Color separations by Reprocolor Llovet, Barcelona, Spain
Printed and bound by Cronion S.A., Barcelona, Spain

Library of Congress Cataloging in Publication Data
Dance: a very social history
    Catalog of an exhibition in the Metropolitan Museum of Art.
    1. Dancing—Social aspects—History—Exhibitions.
2. Costume—History—Exhibitions. 3. Metropolitan Museum of Art (New
York, N.Y.)—Catalogs. I. Wallace, Carol, 1955–. II. Metropolitan Museum of
Art (New York, N.Y.)
GV1588.6.D36 1986 306'.484'07401471 86–28580
ISBN 0–87099–486–7
ISBN 0–8478–0819–X (Rizzoli)

Frontispiece: Photograph of Irene Castle by Cecil Beaton

Contents

Foreword

The Ball nights in Bath are moments snatched from Paradise, rendered bewitching by music, beauty, elegance, fashion, etiquette. . . .

Thus did Charles Dickens in *Pickwick Papers* describe the magic of a grand ball. Even the names of such dances as the minuet, the quadrille, and the waltz are enough to evoke the image of a resplendently dressed assemblage performing with grace and style. The anticipation that precedes such a great social occasion and the afterglow of recollection are intensified not just by the dance and the music but also by the costumes that are so integral a part of the experience. Dance offers a feast for the eye as well as the ear, for it is in response to the grand ball that costume artists have produced some of their most inspired designs. The collections of the Costume Institute of The Metropolitan Museum of Art are especially rich in clothing made expressly for dancing, from the formal gowns of the eighteenth and nineteenth centuries to the mini-dresses of the twentieth.

One of the hallmarks of social dancing is the inexhaustible enthusiasm of its practitioners, who invent opportunities to dance whenever possible—birthday balls, holiday balls, hunt balls, and shipboard balls are but a few examples. Sometimes, as in the Assembly Rooms at Bath during the early nineteenth century, several nights a week were given over to dancing. Everyone who could used to give balls, including Queen Victoria, who in 1842 hosted a masquerade ball for which she dressed as Queen Philippa while her consort, Prince Albert, disguised himself as King Edward III.

As dances have exerted a profound influence on the development of costume, so they have affected the manners and mores of the societies in which they originated, changes that have been subtly but clearly recorded in contemporary paintings and decorative arts. The formal elegance of the eighteenth century, for instance, is nowhere more beautifully reflected than in the work of Antoine Watteau, who captured with paint the delicately patterned and watered silks of the costumes of his dancers as well as the stately geometry of their skirts and bodices. The costumes themselves also reveal a great deal about the periods in which they were worn. Ball gowns of the nineteenth century, with their wide crinolines, for example, seem to be made for waltzing romantically—but with one's partner never closer than arm's length. The dances and costumes of the twentieth century combine the exotic with the daring. Before World War I Irene and Vernon Castle inspired a generation by performing the latest dances, including the Latin American tango, at afternoon *thés dansants*, where skirts rose tantalizingly as the music became livelier. After the war, even shorter skirts were necessitated (or inspired) by the Charleston, the turkey trot, and other scandalous steps adored by all levels of society. No matter how chic these became, however, the full-length ball gown never went out of style. The great gowns created by Christian Dior and Charles James in the 1950s epitomized the ball as the high point of the social season. Making an entrance in one of these embroidered or beaded creations immediately established the wearer's position in society.

As it has in past years, the Museum happily pays homage to the guiding spirit of Diana Vreeland, Special Consultant to the Costume Institute. Her keen eye and lifelong commitment to fashion are again reflected in a judicious and singular selection for this, her fifteenth, annual exhibition of costume. The Museum owes a great debt to her and her entire staff.

Preface

This accompanying publication has profited greatly from the combined expertise of its four authors. Jean Druesedow, Associate Curator in Charge of the Costume Institute, has provided a delightful survey of the costumes, while the iconography of dance as it has been interpreted in the visual arts is analyzed by Laurence Libin, Curator of the Museum's Department of Musical Instruments, assisted by Constance Old. Don McDonagh has sketched for us the evolution of social dances, while Carol Wallace has contributed an anecdotal history of those who performed them. Other individuals whose work has been crucial in producing the book and mounting the exhibition include Katell le Bourhis, Research Associate and coordinator for the exhibition, and Martha Deese, Exhibition Assistant. Together with the authors, Andrew Solomon researched and collected the illustrations for this volume, and Roberta Savage, the designer, has put them together in a manner that reflects the spirit of the subject. I wish to thank Barbara Burn, Executive Editor of the Editorial Department, for her excellent work in developing the book and seeing it through to publication. Special thanks are due also to Reba Adler, Charles Flynn, Coco Flynn, Robert Kauffman, David Kiehl, Joan M. Macri, and Monica Mosley.

Finally, I gratefully acknowledge Valerian Rybar and Jean-François Daigré, who have selflessly contributed their talents to the design concept for the exhibition, and I express my deepest appreciation to Shiseido Cosmetics for the essential support they have so obligingly provided.

Philippe de Montebello
Director
The Metropolitan Museum of Art

Dance is a celebration.

Dance is the vitality and expression that exist in all of us. Throughout history, beautiful and enticing clothes have been made for dancing, because dressing for balls and parties has been the delight of women and men since the beginning of time. The luxurious drama generated by the cut and the exquisite fabric of a dress enhances and echoes the dance movement. Great dresses have a spirit of their own, projecting allure into the wearer and into the evening. A dazzling fantasy is created by lace and chiffon, brocade and lamé, ribbons and paillettes.

Dance and the clothing the world chooses to dance in are a response to the music, to the joy. They are a reflection of how the world was at a particular point in history, or is today. Dance recreates the aura of a time gone by, in the carefully mannered dignity of the minuet, the joy and languor of the waltz, the raucousness of the polka, the high energy of the turkey trot, the seductive insolence of the tango, or the boldness of the twist. Molière said that the destiny of nations depends on the art of dancing, and his words ring true today as one senses the manner and ways of each generation in the dances it produced.

Diana Vreeland
Special Consultant
The Costume Institute

Photograph of evening slipper by Roger Vivier for Dior by Richard Avedon

Introduction

In Japan we have always been impressed with the talent and taste of Diana Vreeland and her ability to produce magnificent costume exhibitions at The Metropolitan Museum of Art. Since her first exhibition, "The World of Balenciaga," in 1972, she has consistently maintained a high level, and we are especially pleased to sponsor "Dance," her fifteenth exhibition.

It is generally believed that the first performance of Western dance in Japan took place in 1883 at a government guest house called the Rokumeikan. The government of that time, after more than two centuries of Japanese isolation, was bent upon absorbing Western culture for the purpose of making Japan a member of the Western community of nations. The Rokumeikan itself became a symbol of Westernism.

While the Rokumeikan was a place of varied social activities, one of its chief functions was to hold formal balls almost every evening for the entertainment of diplomats, senior officials, and guests of the government. Women of the imperial court and upper echelons of society traded their Japanese dress for Western costume—bustle-style gowns that came from Paris. Naturally, all who attended learned dances such as the quadrille, waltz, polka, mazurka, and lancers.

The many events held at the Rokumeikan offered welcome opportunities for the Japanese to assimilate different facets of Western culture, including architecture, music, fashion, cuisine —even etiquette. Japan, long a keen observer of foreign cultures, absorbed and adapted the many customs and mores it was exposed to, resulting in the unique Japanese culture as it is widely known in the world today.

In 1872, eleven years before the opening of the Rokumeikan, Shiseido was established as the forerunner of private Western-style pharmacies in Japan. Evolving as a creator of Western-style cosmetics, Shiseido owed its understanding of modern pharmacology to Shinzo Fukuhara, son of Shiseido's founder, who studied pharmacology as well as fine art in New York and Paris for five years. Upon returning home, he introduced Western aesthetic values to Japan through his cosmetics company and paved the way for Japanese women to dream of Western beauty and glamour. Today Shiseido cosmetics are appreciated in America and around the world as being truly Japanese in spirit.

We at Shiseido are proud to continue this tradition by participating in "Dance," and we hope that people from around the world will enjoy the exhibition and the book that accompanies it.

Yoshio Ohno
President and Chief Executive Officer
Shiseido Co., Ltd.

Dreams of Flight

"The nobility and financiers thus lived in intimacy and in cama-raderie in the garrison and in Parisian society; the balls at Versailles restored the line of demarcation [between aristocrats and the middle class] in the bluntest fashion. Monsieur de Lusson, a young man with a charming face, immensely rich, a good officer, who lived habitually in the best company, had the imprudence to go to one of these balls; he was chased away with such severity that, despairing on account of the ridicule he was covered with in an era when ridicule was the worst of evils, he killed himself on arriving in Paris. This seemed perfectly ordinary to the people of the court, but odious to the haute bourgeoisie."*

—*Comtesse de Boigne*, Mémoires

by Carol McD. Wallace

Twirling figures, gloved hands clasped, the strains of the violin; wilted nosegays, the family jewels, eagerness and flirtation and vanity; matches made, matches broken, gossip repeated and reputations ruined; dancing, dancing badly, dancing too close, dancing like an angel. The upper classes have always danced. They have danced at court fêtes, at public assemblies, at debutante parties, at tea dances, in hotels and nightclubs and at charity balls. They have danced as recreation, for dancing is exhilarating and enjoyable. But behind the stately figures of the minuet or the pulsing of the tango there are—and have always been—other purposes. For a ballroom is a controlled environment; the guests at a ball, having been screened by invitation, presumably all meet the same social standards. Because of this screening, and because men and women meet in a ballroom on an equal footing, opportunities for matchmaking abound.

Of course, because a ball is exclusive, there are also people trying to get in who do not belong. Some succeed, though the equipment for success and the success rate itself vary wildly from country to country, era to era. Overall, the social structure that kept eighteenth-century Versailles and London relatively pure has, needless to say, changed. The waltz, ragtime, and the twist have all been blamed for ushering chaos into the stately environment of the ballroom. So, too, with more reason, have the rise of the middle class, wars, and Freud. Despite the march of modernity, however, people still give balls. The ballrooms in Newport's mansions blaze with light all summer long for this dance or that; marquees mushroom in English gardens during the season; Versailles, from time to time, still vibrates to music. People still want to be invited but are not; romances and marriages are still made and broken. The dance goes on.

1-1. *Opposite:* In 1745 Louis XV and seven courtiers, impenetrably disguised as clipped yew trees, entered the Galerie des Glaces at Versailles for a costume ball. The king used his elaborately achieved anonymity to flirt and dance with one Mme d'Etioles, soon to become famous as his mistress, Mme de Pompadour.

1-2. *Above:* The clipped yew tree, reinterpreted by couturier Paul Poiret, 1912.

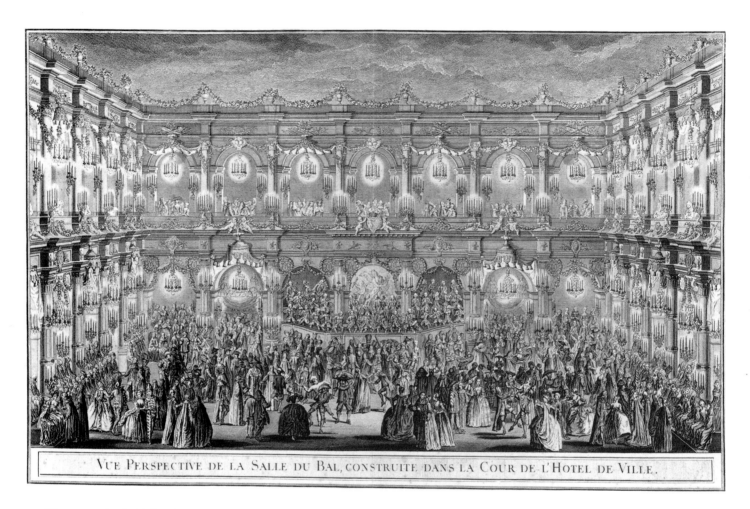

VUE PERSPECTIVE DE LA SALLE DU BAL, CONSTRUITE DANS LA COUR DE L'HOTEL DE VILLE.

1-3. The courtyard at Paris's Hôtel de Ville, converted into an elaborate ballroom for one night's festivities. Boxes for spectators, massive garlands of flowers, and thousands of candles completely transformed the seat of municipal bureaucracy.

The Ancien Régime

For grandeur, in the eighteenth century, nothing could surpass Versailles. The name conjures up images of long, high-ceilinged rooms with glossy parquet floors and gilded paneling. One imagines formal figures, with extravagant panniers and powdered hair, gliding across the floor with a rustle of silk in the characteristic courtier's walk, the *pas de Reine* (the women looked as if they moved on wheels). Candlelight and jewel-spangled fabric, enameled snuffboxes and red-heeled shoes, art and artifice made that world. There, cooped up in a magnificent palace run according to a very strict etiquette, the great nobles of France idled away year after year.

But who would have been elsewhere? Versailles was the seat of fashion and influence, and to be sent away was disgrace. The courtiers of Versailles had the daily satisfaction of knowing that they were in the most excruciatingly exclusive spot in the world—and they spent much of their time and attention on further refining the levels of exclusivity within that world.

It was not enough that, for one to be presented at court, one's family need have been noble since 1400 or performed significant service to the king as a minister, ambassador, or marshal of France. Satisfying though it was to think that the bourgeoisie was shut out from the exquisite life of *ce pays-ci* (as Versailles was known), daily effort went into securing, guarding, or encroaching upon high position. Everyone cared deeply about rank and favor—aside from fashion, these were the principal concerns at Versailles. And every moment of the day provided opportunities to assert one's rank. In chapel, the dukes and princes could provide themselves with cushions to kneel on but only Princes of the Blood could place those cushions at a straight angle on the floor. Who sat in whose presence, who was placed where at table, who danced in which order at a ball—these were matters of enormous moment.

Of course, the balls were numerous. Royal weddings, royal births, victories, all called for protracted series of celebratory balls. Many of these were rigorously exclusive: Horace Walpole, for example, in 1775 attended a ball at Versailles where he considered himself lucky to have been assigned a seat on the *banc des ambassadeurs;* he did not expect to dance, for only royalty and a few chosen nobles did that. It was almost like a performance of a ballet, and Walpole criticized it as such. Walpole, writing to the countess of Upper Ossory, did not think "the clothes, though of gauze and the lightest silks, had much taste," and he said, "I was not so struck with the dancing as I expected." But he thought Marie Antoinette was heavenly, for her beauty and her grace. "The monarch did not dance, but for the two first rounds of the minuets even the Queen does not turn her back to him"; no mean feat when following the highly complex steps of a minuet.

It was a beautiful, hermetic world, but the seal between the French court and the outside world was not complete. There were ambassadors and marshals and ministers sprung from the middle class: the duc de Richelieu, for instance, never lived down his descent from the rather plebeian—albeit brilliant—finance minister Fouquet. Royal mistresses, too, could experience a dizzying elevation in rank and influence with their tenancy of the king's bed. Louis XIV had actually married the strict, religious, and not aristocratically bred Mme de Maintenon.

Then there was the case of Jeanne Poisson, whose story is told with great charm in a biography by Nancy Mitford. Jeanne Poisson was a bourgeoise. She was also, as it happened, charming, beautiful, and talented. She danced, sang, painted, rode, engraved precious stones, and dressed brilliantly, which took a great deal of effort in the 1740s. She was, with all these

extraordinary gifts, a woman of warmth and honesty, straightforward, kind, and generous. She married a M. d'Etioles and became very popular in bourgeois circles in Paris. As a bourgeoise, she could never be presented to France's monarch, so there were distinct limits to her social horizons. She did have a country house near Versailles, however, and it was traditional that neighbors were allowed to follow the king's hunt in carriages. Jeanne could not possibly resist that opportunity; she followed the hunt, one day in a pink dress riding in a blue phaeton, the next day wearing a blue dress in a pink phaeton. The

1-4. The ladies seem hard put to keep their balance during a Scotch reel under their huge coiffures, which were erected over a cushion or a framework of wire, pomaded into place, and then powdered white. These elaborate hairdos were usually undone once a month, and in the interim they often attracted vermin.

1-5. *Left:* The duchess of Devonshire, seen here (*center*) at the Windsor Ball, was the ravishing young wife of one of England's greatest noblemen. Charming, vivacious, and spendthrift, she set the fashions for late-eighteenth-century England, much as Marie Antoinette did in France.

king, handsome, passionate Louis XV, noticed. His mistress, the duchesse de Chateauroux, noticed him noticing, and warned off little Mme d'Etioles.

Then Mme de Chateauroux died. That the king would take a new mistress nobody doubted, and every pretty, ambitious woman in Paris or Versailles imagined herself in the role. Though it was rumored that the king was tired of the plotting and scheming of his aristocratic mistresses, it seemed impossible that any woman of the middle class could fill such an exalted place.

Nevertheless, there were many bourgeoises eager to try. There was one way they could meet the king—at public balls. In the town of Ver-sailles and in Paris, certain balls were open to anyone sufficiently well dressed. The king loved to dance, so he frequently attended these fêtes, but in spite of his mask, his voice and characteristic walk would give him away, and he would be mobbed by lovely if importunate women.

In February of 1745, the dauphin was married, and there were festivities almost every night. Garlands of roses, enormous buffet tables covered in pink velvet, marble walls put up for a night, palm trees, chandeliers, and thousands of candles decked ballrooms in Paris and Versailles. The climax was a masked ball at the palace of Versailles. Every window blazed with light, and

1-6, 7. A less ambitious alternative to a costume was the domino, the loose garment worn *opposite*, and by the lady at the center of the dance floor (*left*). The combination of mask and hooded domino was, for all its simplicity, an effective disguise.

1-8. Bath became a fashionable watering place in the late eighteenth century, and one of its great attractions was the social life. Because many visitors to Bath stayed in small rented houses or inns, they relied on the balls in the assembly rooms for entertainment. Thomas Rowlandson (British, 1756–1827) wittily captured the mood and personality of the place in this drawing of about 1798.

carriages coming from Paris thronged the roads and jammed the courtyard. Balls in the state apartments at Versailles, unlike more exclusive court festivities, were among those open to the properly costumed public, and on this evening Paris had been turned upside down for swords, masks, dominos, shepherdess costumes, real and artificial jewels. Crowds flowed through the Galerie des Glaces and the seven other reception rooms, each of which had its own buffet and band. The queen entered, draped with pearls: the dauphin and the dauphine, unmasked, were costumed as a gardener and a flower seller. Finally, the door to the Oeil de Boeuf opened for the king's entrance, and the crowd shuffled and pressed closer. There emerged, not one man, but eight, costumed identically. The king, to guard his anonymity for one evening, had enlisted seven of his courtiers to be dressed as he was, each in the impenetrable guise of a clipped yew tree.

Which one was the king? One lady put up with a great deal of scratching from twigs, only to find that she had guessed wrong. When one yew tree was seen to devote itself to Mme d'Etioles

(dressed as Diana the huntress), the court drew its conclusions. She would, it seemed, despite her Poisson birth, be the king's next mistress.

He made her the marquise de Pompadour, and she underwent a rigorous indoctrination in court etiquette. Despite her enormous charms, or because of her now-enormous power, she would have enemies at Versailles for the rest of her life, but she made the king happy.

The Romantic Englishman

In the golden age of the aristocracy, Jeanne Poisson had scaled the heights by the only route open to her. A man could be a brilliant soldier or politician; a woman could flutter her fan and bewitch someone powerful. It was not only in France that this was possible; the opportunities were even better in England. For in England, the *mésalliance* was as much an aristocratic tradition as the grand tour.

London of this era was unlike Versailles in

"I had ever so many chances of dancing, but only did 3 times, what with the valses, galops, and being jilted twice."
—*Diary of Lady Frederick Cavendish,*
28 June 1859

that the nobles, and not the king, dominated the social scene. The great aristocratic families had their country estates, and when they came up to town, they stayed in such splendid mansions as Devonshire House and Spencer House. There were myriad balls and myriad scandals, and though everybody who was anybody may have been aware of them all, they took on a sort of independence of one another that never would have been possible in closely regulated France. So eighteenth-century English social history is diffuse and episodic, a great amalgam of remarkable incidents.

The exploits of the Gunning sisters, Maria and Elizabeth, were so extraordinary that Horace Walpole claimed that "the luck of the Gunnings" had become an Irish proverb. He wrote, in a letter to Horace Mann: "These are two Irish girls of no fortune, who are declared the handsomest women alive. I think their being two, so handsome and both such perfect figures, is their chief excellence;...however, they can't walk in the park, or go to Vauxhall, but such mobs follow them that they are generally driven away."

They were not driven away, however, from the house that the earl of Chesterfield had spent five years building in remote Mayfair, one of the most splendid houses in London. With its gardens, its glorious marble staircase, and its French-style moldings and paneling, the house caused enormous excitement. When Lord Chesterfield sent out invitations to what Walpole called "an immense assembly...to show the house which is really most magnificent," all of London society planned to go. The Gunnings had been in London for a year, and Maria had attracted the attentions of the earl of Coventry, a sober young man.

By the evening of Chesterfield's ball, Maria

had very nearly snared her man. Elizabeth, it seemed, had enraptured the duke of Hamilton, "hot, debauched, extravagant, and equally damaged in his fortune and person," at a masquerade at the King's Theatre in Haymarket a month earlier. Elizabeth was to go to Chesterfield's as a sultana, but in the end let Maria have her jeweled costume and went in the simple garb of a Quakeress. This demure clothing did not discourage the duke of Hamilton, however; he was unable to take his eyes off Elizabeth all evening.

Walpole, in another letter to Horace Mann, said, "Duke Hamilton made violent love at one end of the room, while he was playing at pharaoh [faro] at the other end...." He lost a thousand pounds at cards, and his heart as well, for two nights later he found Elizabeth at home alone, her mother and sister having opportunely gone out. Henry Fox wrote, "I fancy he tried what he could do without matrimony. But at one o'clock (not prevailing, I suppose) sent for his friend

1-9. Though France and England might rollick under the reigns of regents and emperors, social America was still in its earnest provincial phase, where early hours and modest entertainments were standard. Waltzing would not reach Fishkill, New York, for decades after this "social ball" took place.

1-10. The young lady at the piano, *below*, has been pressed into service to provide music for the dancers at an American ball about 1815. Perhaps the young men clustered nearby are paying her meaningful compliments on her playing, or perhaps they are only avoiding dancing, as the older set at the card table is doing.

Lord Home out of bed...." The couple was married that night at Mayfair Chapel with, Walpole says, a curtain-ring as a wedding ring; "and what is more silly, my Lord Coventry declares that now he will marry the other." This is precisely what he did.

The Democratic Experiment

As one commentator remarked, America's classes represented the social cake with the icing left off. Careers like those of Mme de Pompadour and the Gunning sisters were virtually impossible since the strong Puritan strain made the concept of mistresses reprehensible. Even dancing had been frowned on; Boston had expelled a dancing teacher as recently as 1686. But democratic idealism could not hold out forever against the deep-rooted human desire to differentiate between classes, and dancing provided an excellent mark of rank. It was wholly nonutilitarian. Furthermore, the complex minuets and country dances of the eighteenth century required study. Study implied leisure, and in the hardworking new republic perhaps nothing seemed more aristocratic than free time.

So Americans, too, took dancing seriously. Thomas Jefferson urged his daughter Martha to practice dancing for three hours every other day—while at "King" Carter's Nomini Hall in Virginia, a Mr. Christian drilled his pupils in the art from breakfast to two in the afternoon and then again from half-past three until dinner. Dixon Wecter, in his splendid *Saga of American*

Society, says the French writer Chateaubriand claimed that the Iroquois Indians retained their own French dancing master, a M. Violet.

Society in the United States was deeply provincial. In a country where very few houses were large enough to contain ballrooms, it was natural that the principal venue for society's revels would be public assemblies. The assembly was an English tradition, popular in such spa towns as Bath, Harrogate, and Tunbridge Wells, where it served as the meeting ground for the social elite, who gave frequent concerts and weekly subscription balls.

Philadelphia, which was probably America's most sophisticated city in the eighteenth century, had its first assembly in 1719, and by 1748 some fifty of the city's "best" families had established the assembly as an annual event. The master of ceremonies, a high-ranking army officer, would assign partners for the evening (by selecting numbered tickets at random), and etiquette had it that one should call on one's partner the following day for a discussion of the evening. The dancing was taken very seriously; young ladies often brought a spare pair of slippers in case they danced through their first, and the marquis de Chastellux, a French visitor at a 1781 assembly, heard the master of ceremonies reprimand a young lady because she had been gossiping and had missed a turn in a country dance: "Come, miss, have a care what you are doing! Do you think you are here for your own pleasure?"

What de Chastellux found even more remarkable about the assembly, however, was how Americans seemed to assign ranks in their ad hoc society. He noticed how the French minister

1-11. Almack's was London's fashionable assembly room, run by a group of patronesses who distributed vouchers for entry only to the best bred and best behaved. Gentlemen who attempted entry in less than correct evening attire were turned away; Regency dandy Beau Brummell, pictured here in 1815, was always impeccably dressed.

"presented his hand to Mrs. Morris, and gave her the precedence, an honor pretty generally bestowed on her, as she is the richest woman in the city, and all ranks here being equal, men follow their natural bent, by giving the preference to riches."

It was the very opposite of what would have happened at the French court or in London, where inherited rank kept society sorted and graded. But the power of wealth—the power, in fact, of the middle class—was gathering strength. In another hundred years, the standards set in provincial Philadelphia would prevail in ballrooms everywhere.

Regency Rakes

Of course, the transition from a society dominated by hereditary aristocrats to one dominated by self-made men was painful, especially in France. Not that the new republicans were without their own pretensions, or that the life of the

ballroom was forgotten. But it took on a macabre tone in the social shambles of the Directoire era, when such excesses as *bals à la victime* appeared. Only blood relatives of guillotine victims were invited, and women wore red ribbons around their throats as an all-too-obvious reminder of the blade. During the dance, one shook one's head back and forth as if it were about to roll off.

Napoleon's imperial phase presented a social dilemma to what was left of aristocratic Paris: did one give in and enjoy the glittering festivities of the Tuileries? It would mean acknowledging not only the upstart Corsican but also his *arriviste* friends, with their new titles and vulgar accents. The pride that had kept the French nobility isolated at Versailles meant that many of them simply retired to their *hôtels particuliers* in the Faubourg Saint-Germain and hibernated during the political and social schizophrenia that continued to convulse France for decades.

In England, the nobility kept their heads and their privileges and at the same time maintained the prerogatives of extravagance that had been theirs in the eighteenth century. Balls were if anything more fabulous and life more scandal-

1-12. In Jane Austen's *Emma* dancing after dinner is proposed one evening. It was "so effectually promoted by Mr. and Mrs. Cole that everything was rapidly cleared away, to give proper space. Mrs. Weston, capital in her country-dances, was seated, and beginning an irresistible waltz; and Frank Churchill, coming up with becoming gallantry to Emma, had secured her hand."

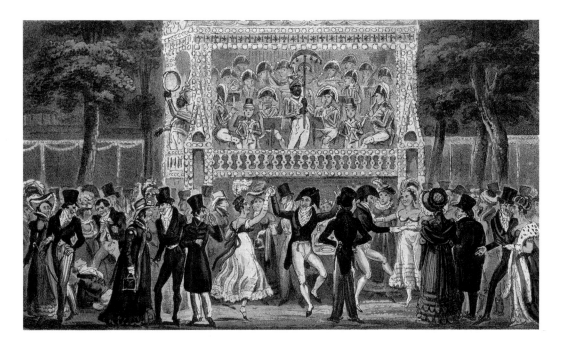

1-13. *Left*: During an evening's romp at London's Vauxhall Gardens, here depicted by George Cruikshank (British, 1792–1878), ladies and gentlemen of every degree of virtue mingle. The gown of the lady dancing at the right is decolleté, diaphanous, and displays several inches of ankle, indicating her lack of respectability.

1-14. *Below left*: When the young and handsome Prince of Wales visited New York in 1860, the American reception was overwhelmingly enthusiastic. Nearly a thousand uninvited guests joined the four thousand legitimate ones at the October 12 ball, and the floor of the Academy of Music collapsed (and was hastily repaired) just before His Royal Highness's entrance. Though some of his suite did not approve of the New York ladies' manners, the prince reportedly eluded his chaperons and spent the hours after the ball in a brothel.

1-15. *Opposite*: In this painting, *La Soirée* (1880) by Jean Béraud (French, 1849–1936), the young ladies are "sitting out" between dances in the respectable presence of a gray-haired dowager, while the men in the doorway survey the goods on display. If the young lady in the foreground is not related to the gentleman sitting behind her (and if he sits there for much longer), she can be classified as a terrible flirt.

ous, given the enthusiastic example set by the prince regent.

It was hard to go too far in Regency society, but Lord Byron's liaison with Lady Caroline Lamb was to shock everyone. It became a very public affair in London's salons and ballrooms for most of a summer season. But Byron tired of Lady Caroline, and when English society dispersed to its country houses, he did not regret the parting. They corresponded, he temperately, she despairingly, and finally met again at a ball in London in July of 1813. Caroline was already there when Byron arrived with his new mistress, Lady Oxford (formerly Caroline's best friend). Caroline had been an aficionado of the waltz before her affair but had stopped dancing in deference to Byron's lameness. Now, as the band broke into a waltz, she defiantly seized a partner and began to dance. When, in the supper room later, Byron made a sarcastic comment to her, she broke a glass, as her somewhat skeptical mother-in-law Lady Melbourne told the story, "and scratched herself...with the broken pieces."

1-16. *Above*: Mrs. Cornelius Vanderbilt pays homage to a modern invention in this "Electric Light" ensemble, created by the Parisian couturier Worth in 1883 for sister-in-law Alva Vanderbilt's fancy-dress ball. The evening marked the Vanderbilts' hard-won arrival at the peak of New York society.

1-17. *Right*: Cavaliers, duchesses, and milkmaids cavorted at the William K. Vanderbilt ball of 1883. The hostess was dressed as a Venetian princess, her husband as the duc de Guise. The house—for the ball was also a housewarming—was permanently costumed as a French château.

1-18. *Opposite*: From the potted palms to the gentleman's gloves to the tip of the debutante's white slipper, this painting, *La Danse à la Ville*, by Pierre-Auguste Renoir (French, 1841–1919) is a vision of a perfectly correct evening in a Parisian *hôtel particulier*.

Lady Caroline Lamb's devotion to the waltz was entirely typical of her, in that it bordered on impropriety. The seductive music and the scandalously close embrace of the dance made it very slow to catch on in conservative society. The 1814 opening of the Congress of Vienna was one of the first occasions at which the waltz was the dominant dance, and even the British foreign secretary, Lord Castlereagh, realized he would have to give in and learn it. Susan Mary Alsop, in *The Congress Dances*, tells how he and his wife hired a dancing teacher when they arrived in Vienna for the congress, and Lord Castlereagh was rumored to practice with a chair when his wife was not available.

The work of the congress went slowly, but the social pace was frantic, involving as it did international competition. The Austrians, English, and Russians entertained as lavishly as their country's governments could afford. Emperor Francis I of Austria gave a masked ball for ten thousand at the Hofburg; Princess Catherine Bagration, the czar's mistress, gave a select ball for two hundred at the Palm Palace. Metternich and his wife gave a ball at their country villa to which guests were supposed to wear native costume; Lady Castlereagh interpreted indigenous English garb by wearing her husband's Order of the Garter in her hair. Her whimsicality was condemned as irreverence, a typical reaction to the outré behavior that was to become common currency as the century went on.

The Age of Reason had given way to the Romanticism of the early nineteenth century, which was in turn growing into the sentimentality and prurience of the Victorians. The currents of reform that were in the air were accompanied by a spirit of prudishness and restraint. The French Revolution had taught a lesson of sorts to some noble families, who instituted family prayers and a life of respectability—a concept that would have aroused contempt in the rollicking aristocrats of the eighteenth century. In 1802 a man named Thomas Bowdler published an expurgated ver-

sion of Shakespeare with all the nasty bits removed. The regent became king, married, and produced a legitimate child. In 1819 the duke of Kent (George III's fourth son) had a daughter named Victoria. In eighteen years, she would be queen, and the golden age for heedless aristocrats would be over.

The Machinery of Society

The period has taken on her name, but in many ways Queen Victoria reflected rather than originated its zeitgeist. Earnest, sober, hardworking, pious, she regarded even the English aristocrats with misgiving, finding them dissolute and frivolous. But though the bankers and industrialists of the nineteenth century agreed with her, they nevertheless wanted to imitate the aristocratic style. They sent their sons to Eton, bought estates from broken-down nobles, and swanned around Mayfair with the best of them, but they needed a little help. Hence the flood of etiquette books that interpreted such arcana as how many cards to leave when calling on a married lady, precisely when to switch to half-mourning, and how to introduce a duchess to a bishop. In America, the hunger for gentility was even greater and more urgent. Society was constantly amused by those postulants to the beau monde who had not studied quite carefully enough the manners of those they emulated.

Behind the amusement, however, was fear. In America the standard of class was pecuniary. People may have fussed about old money and good breeding, but new money became old money with lightning speed. Numerous barriers were erected against the incursion of the most newly wealthy—lists, clubs, private assemblies —but an elaborate code of etiquette was one of the most effective. Mismanaging any of the details of polite life efficiently branded the outsiders. As one manual of the era, *Social Etiquette of New York*, stated coolly, "Etiquette is the machinery of society. It polishes and protects even while conducting its charge. It prevents the agony of uncertainty. . . . If one is certain of being correct, there is little to be anxious about."

It seems hard to believe. Even before a lady going to a ball had left the house, she had to be anxious about her dress, hair, gloves, fan, bouquet in its posy-holder, skirt-lifter, carnet de bal,

and hand-cooler. Then there was the additional encumbrance of the chaperon. The chaperon—a mother, elderly relative, or sedate married friend—was a familiar figure in French and English ballrooms, and growing social pretensions imported her to the East Coast of America by the middle of the nineteenth century. (She never did penetrate the western wilds.) As Mrs. Sherwood wrote in her 1884 volume on etiquette, the chaperon "must watch the characters of the men who approach her charge, and endeavor to save the inexperienced girl from the dangers of a bad marriage, if possible." Unmarried girls were accompanied everywhere by a chaperon: to the theater, to buy a new hat, to go visiting, and certainly to a dance. Even there, a chaperon was separated from her charge only when the latter was actually swept off to perform a country dance or a quadrille. The young lady was returned promptly to the supervision of the matron, and if the young man wished to chat, he did so *à trois*.

So a lady would go off to a ball in the 1880s, hung about with her little trinkets and accompanied by her chaperon. She would arrive at her destination, a vast house blazing with light, carriages crowding outside, a red carpet and awning leading up to the steps. She would leave her wraps in a dressing room and proceed to where her hostess and host were receiving. An impressive manservant would announce her name, she would curtsy and move into the ballroom. The band was often invisible, hidden in a musicians' gallery or screened by a bower of potted palms. Little gilded chairs lined the sides of the room, and plaques, ropes, or pyramids of flowers covered the walls, twined in the chandeliers, looped the frames of windows and mirrors. One arrived late at a ball, after having been at the opera or a dinner or another ball; dancing would be well under way. One found one's friends, gentlemen requested dances, one danced a bit. The music stopped near midnight as a signal that supper had been served, and the company moved to the supper room where, at small tables, they were served by footmen. After supper, the cotillion or german would begin.

The cotillion was an elaborate country dance which could last as long as four hours. A partnerless master of ceremonies managed the intricate dance figures as they succeeded each other. The dance always involved favors, such as flowers or ribbons, passed out to the men and women, who would then, in the course of the dance, give them to their partners. Many of the figures of the dance entailed choosing a new partner, who would then receive a new favor. The "mirror figure" featured a girl sitting in a chair in the middle of the dance floor, holding up a mirror. One by one, men would dance toward her and show their faces in the mirror. She would wipe away their images with a handkerchief until the one she wanted presented himself. In the "fan figure" men and women were separated by a six-foot fan, and ladies fluttered diminutive versions over the edge of the large fan. The men chose the color they liked best. The "butterfly figure" had men literally chasing ladies around the dance floor with butterfly nets, while the "four-in-hand" had men "driving" quartets of women (decked with bells) around the ballroom in a prancing step. Maude Howe Elliott, a Newport debutante, recalled in *This Was My Newport* that "girl or boy, your success depended on the number of times you were taken out," or chosen as a partner. The accumulation of favors, worn on the shoulders or piled on a chair, was a badge of achievement.

Not all ladies, of course, were popular, and they might not even have emerged from supper with a partner for the cotillion. Worse, they might not have found a man to take them to supper. In theory, the gentleman who had partnered the lady for the previous dance should escort her, but he might be otherwise engaged. (Whim had nothing to do with the lady's accepting; as one manual put it, "A ball is too formal a place for any one to indulge in personal preference of any kind.") Or the lady might not have danced that last dance. She could not go down to supper without a male partner and in fact had to leave the ball if one did not materialize. If she did have a supper partner, she then had to rely utterly on him to see that she was served properly.

A woman sitting alone with her plate of chicken croquettes would have seemed terribly forward. In fact, women had to contend not only with their fans and bouquets and impedimenta, but with a bewildering array of proscriptions, lest they be thought "fast." *Punch* described the behavior of the Victorian flirt: "The mere shade, the very idea of a gentle pressure of the hand as she meets you in the chain of the last figure of the Lancers induces you to believe yourself the favoured one. She is very fond of going down to refreshment: it removes her from the espionage of her chaperon. She sits on the staircase outside the drawing room door under pretence of enjoying the cool air."

1-21. Lady Randolph Churchill (Winston's mother) was one of the three lovely Jerome sisters from Brooklyn, all of whom married English aristocrats and shared a taste for Worth dresses. When Lord Randolph was secretary of state for India, Queen Victoria presented Jennie with the Order of the Crown of India, whose insignia she wears on her left shoulder. It is set with pearls and turquoises and worn on a turquoise ribbon, and Jennie promptly had Worth make this dress to match it.

27

1-22. Though the proceedings look tame enough, this ball for the centennial of George Washington's inauguration was actually something of a shambles. Very large, and "semi-public," it attracted an element unfamiliar to most New York ballrooms. The New York *Times* reported that when the supper rooms opened, "the food was scattered everywhere indiscriminately—on the ladies' costumes and on the walls."

The idea was that young ladies were pure and men were wolves. However, no wolf would want to take a less-than-pure young girl as his wife. In order for a girl to find a husband, she had to be exposed to as many eligible young men as possible without taking any of the bloom off her reputation. This process was known as her "debut."

The Girls in White

The French in particular took this seriously. Young girls in France were educated in convents and closely supervised; their mothers chose their reading matter, read their correspondence, and selected their clothes and their friends. Elisabeth de Gramont, duchesse de Clermont-Tonnerre, wrote in her autobiography, *Pomp and Circumstance*, "There were special concoctions designed for the young girls of our nation. Everything stupid, conventional, factitious, and ugly was set aside for them: fatuous tunes, silly plays, tame conversation, disgusting clothes. Good girls were dressed in light, insipid colors and the poorest of materials, and all the touches that give 'tone'—diamonds, powder, paint, and perfume—were rigorously forbidden." French debutantes were presented to society and danced at *bals blancs*, which were the sole province of unmarried girls. At a party given by Mme de Clermont-Tonnerre's parents, one mother dragged her daughter away because "there were married women at this ball!" Consuelo Vanderbilt, the American heiress, made her debut at a party given for Elisabeth de Gramont, and describes in her memoirs, *The Glitter and the Gold*, her white tulle dress from Worth, her gloves, the narrow ribbon around her neck. "A *bal blanc*," she remembered, "had to live up to its name of purity and innocence; it could not inspire the mild flirtations of a pink ball where young married women were included. The men who attended them, no doubt with the intention of selecting a future spouse, were expected to behave with circumspection. There was no opportunity for conversation. A debutante was invited to dance, and once the dance was over she was escorted back to her mama."

Consuelo's mother, Mrs. William K. Vanderbilt, was enormously ambitious. She wanted her daughter to marry a European title, which, given the Vanderbilt fortune and Consuelo's charms, seemed a reasonable goal. So after rejecting five marriage proposals on Consuelo's behalf, she took her daughter off to London. Here Mrs. Vanderbilt put Consuelo in the hands of Mrs. Arthur Paget, an old friend from New York. Consuelo found her terrifying: "The simple dress I was wearing, my shyness and diffidence which in France were regarded as natural in a debutante, appeared to awaken her ridicule."

Minnie Paget was a great friend (and rumored ex-mistress) of Albert Edward, the Prince of Wales. His set, the fashionable coterie of the wealthy and dashing in England, had very worldly tastes, and if Consuelo was to "take" as a debutante in England, she would have to shed the *jeune fille à marier* image. As she recalled, "Tulle must give way to satin, the baby *décolletage* to a more generous display of neck and arms, naïveté to sophistication."

Consuelo Vanderbilt made her debut in 1894. The strictness of the Victorian age had not relaxed, but the level of luxury had escalated enormously. A ball was still a formal entertainment for several hundred people, but more money was poured into every aspect. Suppers became more elaborate, featuring lobsters and terrapin and endless champagne. Cotillion favors were no longer ribbons and bows, but elaborate and valuable tokens, costing as much as ten thousand dollars each. At a dance given by Mrs. George Gould in New York, the favors were jeweled pins, charms, and rings for the women and scarf-pins for the men. The music was supplied by two or even three orchestras, hired perhaps from the opera for a night. Dresses and jewels were richer and more elaborate; there was even a point when it became the fashion for American ladies to wear tiaras copied from the royal crowns of Europe. Count Boni de Castellane gave a ball in the Bois de Boulogne to celebrate the twenty-first birthday of his wife, Anna Gould: it featured the entire corps de ballet of the Paris Opéra, eighty thousand Venetian glass lamps swinging in the trees, fifteen kilometers of carpet, and sixty footmen in red liveries grouped together to add a bit of color.

With the extravagance came a kind of silliness. Because the forms of entertaining—indeed, the forms of all social life—were so rigid,

1-23. A group pauses to show off their costumes at the princesse de Léon's masquerade ball. The hostess is seated at the center of the group, while another famous host, Count Boni de Castellane, is second from right in a sable-trimmed cloak. One great charm of fancy-dress balls in this era was that guests could wear all their jewels at once without inviting charges of ostentation.

1-24. *Overleaf*: The French took very seriously the task of protecting young girls from the tarnish of male influence. Although when they were officially "out," debutantes could dance with male partners, the kind of entertainment pictured in this painting, *Bal Blanc* by Joseph-Marius Avy (French, 1871–?), seemed a great deal safer for simple recreation.

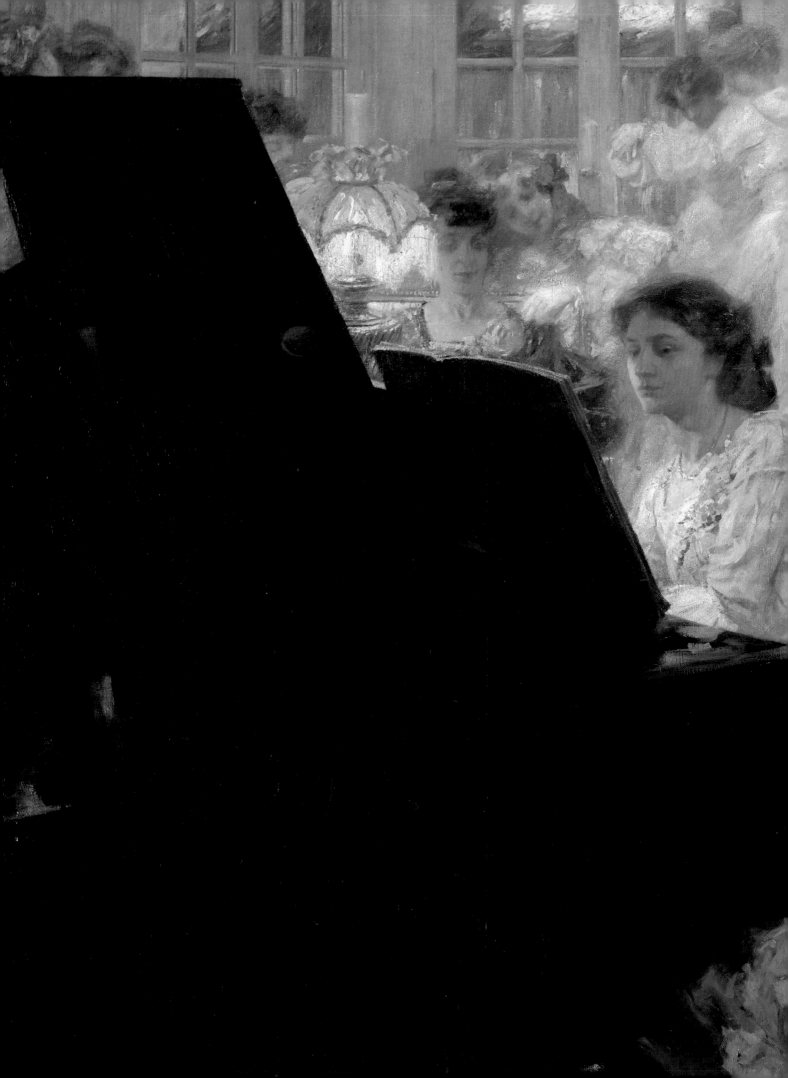

"...my father thought it the sign of a cad and a bounder if a man had worn suede shoes or had shiny buttons (instead of braid ones) at the back of his tail coat and on his sleeves."

—Loelia, Duchess of Westminster
Grace and Favour

1-25. The white dress ornamented with flowers, the discreet string of pearls, the simple hair, and frank glance are perennial debutante attributes. Only a Boston girl of the 1890s would have felt it necessary to add the book.

1-26. *Opposite*: Minnie Paget was dressed by Worth as Cleopatra for the 1897 Devonshire House ball. Her identification with the Egyptian intriguer was appropriate, for she was reputed to have engineered many of the era's matches between impecunious British peers and ambitious American heiresses.

details had to provide the novelty for each party. William C. Whitney gave a coming-out dance for his niece where the cotillion included an "automobile figure": a car, laden with favors, drove onto the ballroom floor. Mrs. Cornelius Vanderbilt gave an "at home" at Newport that involved closing down and bringing to Rhode Island for one night a popular Broadway show. Lest the guests be bored, there was also a ball, a circus midway, a supper, and a sunrise breakfast. James Hazen Hyde turned Sherry's into Versailles, brought the actress Réjane over from Paris, and charged the whole party to the Equitable Life Assurance Company, which he had inherited from his father. A guest entered a New York ballroom in a small cart drawn by a trained seal; at Newport, the most exclusive set gave a "servants' ball" where they impersonated their own maids, valets, and butlers.

Masquerade Madness

Pretending you were someone else was one of the great amusements of the era. Costume balls had long been popular; they were featured at the Congress of Vienna; they were a staple of the *louche* side of Regency life, with heavily disguised rakes making passes at dominoed ladies in boxes at Vauxhall Gardens. It was precisely that opportunity for sexual license that brought into question the propriety of the form during the early Victorian period—in New York a young couple eloped after a costume ball in 1840, and no one doubted that the evening's revelry contributed to their rashness.

Queen Victoria gave a lavishly spectacular

masquerade ball in May of 1842. She represented Queen Philippa, and Albert was Edward III, while many of their courtiers came as other fourteenth-century celebrities. Though the queen did not leave the ballroom until quarter to three, it was a stately occasion and not to be confused with the sort of party where kisses were snatched in dark corners.

Prudishness and puritanism relaxed, however, and as the century progressed costume balls became ever more frequent. The Prince of Wales gave a fancy-dress ball in 1874 for which Lord Leighton supervised the decor. The prince himself went as Charles I in a fair-haired wig and a black hat trimmed with white ostrich plumes and diamonds, and was thought to look terribly dashing.

The degree of wishful thinking expressed in individual costumes was almost poignant. Americans chose Louis XV, Louis XVI, and Marie Antoinette as perennial favorites; Mrs. Bradley Martin, a matron from upstate New York, actually wore a ruby necklace that had belonged to the doomed queen of France to her own costume ball in 1897. Mary Stuart was popular among romantics who looked pretty in black; ladies who wanted to load on the jewels might choose Elizabeth I. It was important, too, to select a character who could be plausibly dressed in the currently fashionable tight bodice and full, heavy skirt: Empress Josephine would not do, though Cleopatra appeared fairly often in whalebone and satin.

The memoirs of the period describe some of the landmark balls: the William K. Vanderbilt ball of 1883 that marked the Vanderbilts' arrival at the peak of New York society; a Louis XVI ball at Warwick Castle, after which the hostess, Daisy, countess of Warwick, became a socialist; the Bradley Martin ball in New York, for which

event the Waldorf decided to wall up its windows to prevent anarchists from throwing bombs. But the grandest, in the way that only the English could manage by the turn of the century, was the Devonshire House ball in 1897.

It was the year of Queen Victoria's Diamond Jubilee, and the London season had never been so festive. From the debutantes making their bows at court to the languid sprigs of fashion lounging in the window of Brooks's to the Indian nawabs who had come to pay their respects, everyone was conscious of just how splendid it all was. And at Devonshire House, the massive gray William Kent mansion with its great forecourt on Piccadilly and its gardens stretching behind, the duke and duchess were planning their contribution to the splendor. They had married just five years previously, after an affair of such long standing that it became respectable, even though Duchess Louise was married at the time to the duke of Manchester. When she was widowed, their liaison was finally made legitimate, and she was known afterward as the Double Duchess.

On 2 July, the duke with his Victorian beard clambered into his Charles V costume, while the duchess arrayed herself as Zenobia, Queen of Palmyra. Sophia Murphy, in *The Duchess of Devonshire's Ball*, tells how the eight hundred guests had been organized into *entrées*, groups whose costumes were thematically related and who made a ceremonial entrance together. The marchioness of Londonderry was Empress Maria Theresa wearing the massive Londonderry tiara known as the "family fender." Lady Raincliffe represented Catherine the Great, and in her suite were the duke and duchess of Marlborough as the French ambassador to her court and his wife; the duchess, the former Consuelo Vanderbilt, was seven months pregnant, though

1-27. One of the greatest beauties of the Belle Epoque in France, the Comtesse Greffuhle was one of Marcel Proust's models for both the duchesse de Guermantes and the princesse de Guermantes in *A la Recherche des Temps Perdu*. She was also one of the couturier Worth's most inspiring clients, as is amply demonstrated by this gown.

"Tilly Losch asked me to help with her costume for the Oriental Ball. It soon became my work of the morning. Endless telephoning. What is the address of the woman who is so good at make-up? Daisy would know but is away. Iya knows it, Iya is away. Boris would know, or Natasha, or Nabokoff..."

"After creating her costume the whole morning I said 'Now you are complete. All you have to do for the Ball is glue a sequin between your brows.' Tilly whimpered, 'But how can I do that? Won't you come to the hotel and bring some glue?'"

—Cecil Beaton,
diary entry, summer of 1935

"Naturally there have been people who have said that I gave these fêtes as an item of advertisement, but I want to destroy this insinuation, which can only have originated in stupidity."
—*Paul Poiret,*
King of Fashion

1-28. The sleeping figure here may be a caricature of Paul Poiret, whose exotic "1002nd Night" party set the pace for pre–World War I fancy-dress balls. The whaleboned dignity of the nineteenth century has completely vanished.

Pierre Brissaud 1912

"Dancing was going on from the bottom to the top of every home, on waxed floors, on black rugs, beneath lights that were increasingly veiled. Even people who loathed dancing, gave dances."
—Elisabeth de Gramont,
Duchesse de Clermont-Tonnerre
Years of Plenty

1-29. *Below*: With the dancing crazes of the 1910s and 1920s came a rush of attention to technique. The Arrow Shirt man, naturally, is unassailably correct, down to his gloved grasp of the young lady's fingertips.

1-30. *Opposite*: Irene Castle's girlish charm and evident respectability made many frightening fashions— bobbed hair, slit skirts, the tango— seem positively reassuring.

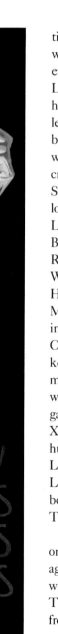

tightly corseted under her sea-green silk. There was an Arthurian *entrée*, an Elizabethan *entrée*, even Louis XV and Louis XVI *entrées*, led by Lady Warwick in the dress she had had made for her own Louis XVI ball. The Oriental *entrée* was led by the hostess, carried in a palanquin borne by fan-wielding slaves. The Prince of Wales wore knee breeches, a ruff, a huge diamond cross, and a cape as grand prior of the Order of St. John of Jerusalem; Princess Alexandra, as lovely as ever, went as Marguerite of Valois. Lady Randolph Churchill (née Jennie Jerome of Brooklyn) was the Empress Theodora of the Roman Empire in a stiffly brocaded robe by Worth, while the countess of Westmoreland was Hebe with a large stuffed eagle on her shoulder. Many of the guests were prevented from dancing by their costumes; the prince of Saxe-Coburg wore a suit of armor and valiantly tried to keep the visor down in the cause of verisimilitude, but the heat defeated him. Supper was served in a tent erected near the pond in the garden; the art dealer Duveen had loaned Louis XIV tapestries, the ground was carpeted, and huge chandeliers lit the palm-decked tables. Late in the evening a crusader and a courtier of Louis XV argued over a woman and actually began sparring, as both happened to be armed. The crusader, with a broadsword, prevailed.

It was an extraordinary evening, and everyone knew there would never be anything like it again. They did not know, however, that the world would soon change as completely as it did. The first inkling of the new dispensation came from America.

Ragtime

It was only a new style of music, but it sounded

1-31. *Above*: After World War I, dancing moved into public venues. The most elegant nightclubs were as exclusive as any ballroom, although a night on the town begun at Paris's Florida might easily finish in bohemian Montmartre.

1-32. *Opposite*: Margot Tennant was the strong-willed daughter of a Scottish baron who made a notable debut in London society and married prominent politician Herbert Asquith. Her brusque, outspoken manner and haughty looks made her many enemies. Nancy Astor used to carry a set of false teeth in her evening bag as an accessory for her Margot Asquith imitation.

suspiciously like anarchy, and the dances it brought in its wake were thought to be undignified and vulgar. In the summer of 1910 the turkey trot was all the rage in Newport among the young people, and however much Mrs. Vanderbilt might hate the new dances, they could not be swept into the primeval mire whence they had indubitably come.

What these new steps lacked was gentility, but they became genteel when Vernon and Irene Castle performed them. Sleek, fair-haired, English Vernon and elegant, vivacious Irene were clearly "our kind, dear." She was the daughter of a New Rochelle doctor, and he had been educated in England as an engineer. They had been stranded nearly penniless in Paris and had taken a job dancing in a Paris café. The Parisians loved them; how could New Yorkers snub them? When they came back to the United States and opened a dancing school and a night-

club, they set fashion after fashion. Irene's flowing dresses that let her move gracefully, her bobbed hair, and her little lace caps were copied instantly. And she and Vernon popularized such dances as the one-step, the Castle Walk, and the tango, making even this sultry mating ritual look perfectly charming on the parquet floor of a Fifth Avenue ballroom.

Waltzes and quadrilles and cotillions had held sway for three quarters of a century, along with dance cards and chaperons and visiting cards. It took the Castles' charismatic yet reassuring quality to interpret the new dances to a hesitant audience. At the same time, society had not welcomed other facets of the twentieth century, accepting only motorcars and the telephone. New currents in the arts went largely ignored or scorned, until some of them, too, were brought into fashion, notably by couturier Paul Poiret.

Poiret embraced the new wholeheartedly, whether in fashion or in art. Among his friends were such artists as van Dongen and Dunoyer de Segonzac, who helped him create settings for his parties. Even Isadora Duncan danced at a Poiret fête. Though he gave numerous elaborate parties, none was more famous than the 1002nd Night, which was to bring orientalia resoundingly into fashion.

The guests—a select three hundred—were invited to come as ancient Persians. Lest they attempt to infiltrate the party in less than authentic garb, Poiret had, as he put it in his memoirs, "a squad of old gentlemen in evening dress, who were no jokers," examining arrivals. The uncooperative were sent upstairs to don extra costumes Poiret had on hand: "I knew the carelessness of some of my friends, and I had taken measures to counteract it." The Faubourg Saint-Honoré mansion had been disguised as effectively as the guests, with tapestries shrouding the windows, tents, fountains, courtyards covered with sand, even an immense golden cage where the sultan's favorite woman was confined. The sultan, needless to say, was Poiret himself, who received his guests sitting on a green and gold throne, dressed in a jeweled turban and a gray caftan trimmed with skunk fur. When all his guests had assembled he opened the door to the cage and the favorite— Mme Poiret—stepped out, revealing her costume of pantaloons and a short, hooped tunic which ladies requested the next day at the Poiret salon as the "lampshade tunic."

The host had exorcised every trace of Paris from his house. Oriental rugs carpeted stairs and courtyards; exotic blue and purple fruit hung from the trees. Braziers burning incense dotted the garden, which was alive with parrots, macaws, peacocks, flamingos, and ibis. There were strolling musicians, dancers, sweetmeat sellers, and strange Eastern foods and liqueurs. A fortune teller, a potter, a pythoness, and a monkey merchant hung all over with tiny, chattering marmosets entertained the crowd. In one long, dark, cavernous room the only light came from the illuminated bottles of liqueurs. Slaves and houris lounged conspicuously on cushions scattered on the ground, ignoring the fireworks that frightened the monkeys so much that they broke their chains and scampered over the roofs of the neighboring houses.

The phantasmagoria of the 1002nd Night was a far cry from the Devonshire House ball, and when a *Vogue* reporter asked couturier Charles Worth what he thought of the new fashions Poiret had launched that night, Worth called the style "vulgar, wicked, and ugly!" But Worth—who had made many of the costumes for the London ball—was a man of the Old World. He was fighting a rear-guard action. Mrs. Stuyvesant Fish, one of Newport's grandes dames, gave a fairy dance in 1913, and though it smacked a bit more of the wholesome American character (with a witch on a broomstick flying through the ballroom and black cats, hobgoblins, and sheaves of wheat as decorations) the Poiret influence was evident in Natalja Willard's rose-trimmed lampshade tunic. *Harper's Bazar* even ran, a few months later, a series of photographs of Oriental costumes that had graced sundry New York balls. Turbans, tunics, and pantaloons were omnipresent that season.

The Jazz Age

World War I did not necessarily bring a halt to dancing. Though the social scene petered out in war-ravaged Paris, in London a shadow of the season went on as usual—or nearly. Lady Diana Cooper would go from assisting at an operation in the hospital temporarily occupying her parents' house to a ball in one of the few houses still open for socializing. A rich American rancher named George Gordon Moore was so entranced by Lady Diana that he gave a series of dances for her, featuring jazz bands and champagne and

1-33. The three illustrations above were first published in *Eve: The Lady's Pictorial* in 1925.

heaps of flowers. They were dubbed "dances of death," since there was no telling who would be alive when the next one was given.

Considering that atmosphere and the extraordinary mortality rate in both the French and English upper classes, it was no wonder that the parties after the war had a very different tone. Before 1914, luxury and beauty and looking divine were still crucial considerations, even to the more progressive socialites like Poiret. After the war, being amusing was all that counted. A woman like Elsa Maxwell was a purely postwar phenomenon.

She was fat and she was plain and she came from nothing. But Elsa Maxwell could give brilliant parties. They were full of surprises, and no one was permitted to stand on his dignity: dignity was at a discount in the twenties. Georgina Howell's *In Vogue* lists Maxwell's seven rules for a good evening's fun, the first of which was ruthlessness about the guest list (no lame ducks). Then, she said, guests should not be allowed to do what they want but should be made to do something entirely different. Rooms should be too crowded, too bright, and noisy. The host should never appear uneasy about how the party is going, but should try to stir up some enmity in the room. And *voilà*, things would go swimmingly.

One of her most famous fêtes was a Parisian come-as-you-were evening; guests were pledged to arrive in the state they were in when the invitation (hand delivered, at unexpected hours of the day) had reached them. Lest they be embarrassed by taking public transport to the party, buses with cocktail bars were provided. It was just as well; there were women in slips, men in hairnets, a lady with exactly half of her face made up, a gentleman in evening dress but without his trousers, and another in his dressing gown with half of his face shaved, the other half still covered with shaving cream.

Not all of the costume balls of the era stressed irreverence to the exclusion of elegance. Comte Etienne de Beaumont gave a famous costume ball with a different theme each year. In 1929 the theme was opera, and from ten until midnight various *entrées* entertained the rest of the guests who were dining. The Faust *entrée* featured a fat man singing falsetto, dressed as Marguerite in blue satin and a yellow wig. The Valkyrie *entrée* was so striking it had to do an encore, and the Moulin Rouge *entrée* included Comte Armand de la Rochefoucauld as the *moulin* itself with a windmill on his head. At midnight all the guests went outside to watch the fireworks, and in the garden certain guests were dressed up as exotic shrubs—a recurring motif in the French imagination, perhaps. The same season, the vicomte and vicomtesse de Noailles gave a party to which their guests were to wear materials not usually used for clothing. They came in rubber and raffia, celluloid and wood, rope, paper, mica, and tin. One couple in marbleized oil cloth were marble statues; Mme Eloui Bey wore a Lelong dress made of pieces of mirror.

Through the twenties and thirties, the costume fever continued in both Paris and London. Elsa Maxwell and Daisy Fellowes gave a party to which the guests had to come as someone everyone else knew; Cecil Beaton was Elinor Glyn and Chanel got a rush of business from young men who wanted gowns to dress up as ladies about town. At the duchesse de Clermont-Tonnerre's, Princesse Violette Murat brought in an *entrée* that was a Harlem wedding party; she was the mother of the bride. English parties were no tamer. At the duke and duchess of Sutherland's in 1926, the marquess of Blandford was a female English Channel swimmer, Lord Birkenhead

1-34. *Left*: Not all nightclubs were elegant, and during Prohibition speakeasies and other dens of iniquity became popular. The kind of place painted here by Howard Thain (American, born 1891) was out of bounds—and thus doubly appealing—to debutantes and girls of good family.

1-35. *Right*: Following in the steps of Irene Castle, Mrs. Blaine Mallon, a young society matron and Junior League member in Washington, D.C., rehearses the tango step that she and her partner, Mr. Paul Wrangel, plan to perform at the Junior League Patchwork Ball.

1-36. *Below*: An illustration from *La Gazette de Bon Genre*, 1921.

was Captain Hook, Lady Diana Cooper was a French revolutionary, and the hostess began the evening dressed in feathers and ended as a wooden soldier. Her thunder was stolen, however, by the eight ladies who "rowed" into the ballroom—boat and all—as the Eton crew, coxed by Duff Cooper. Finally, in 1939, Mrs. Louise Macy gave a ball in Paris at the Hôtel Sâlé. Janet Flanner, writing for *The New Yorker*, called it "the most inventive and best big party" of the season. Guests were requested "to wear diadems and decorations, and no nonsense about their not having any." Finally, the conventional garb of the nineteenth century had itself become a costume.

Hotels, Nightclubs, and Places of Ill Repute

The war had changed more than sartorial habits, and the new dances popularized by the Castles did not remain the new dances for long. In fact, after the war society everywhere underwent a dancing craze, what Loelia, duchess of Westminster, in her memoir *Grace and Favour*, called "the aftermath of the short-leave-from-France frenzy." During the war, soldiers on leave had been privileged beings. If they wanted to dance at teatime, then society girls were more than willing to oblige. If they wanted to hold a young lady closer than she was used to being held, how could she say no?

It made mothers very nervous to have their daughters dancing in public places. No matter that the Ritz was ultrasafe, and that one could not get into much trouble fox-trotting around while the Lapsang Souchong cooled in the teacups. It was the nightclubs that were more worrisome, and perhaps with good reason. In New York, Prohibition cramped the legitimate style and made thrills a little decadent. "Slumming" in Harlem often topped off an evening begun sedately enough at the Four Hundred. In Paris, similarly, a dancing evening might start at a glossy club such as Florida and end up in Montmartre at Le Boeuf sur le Toit.

Some of the nightclubs were actually members' clubs, like, for example, the famous Embassy Club in London. The decor—big mirrors, bright lights, and red banquettes—was unimaginative, but the food and wine were impeccable, and the band, led by Bert Ambrose, was "the best in London," according

1-37. *Opposite*: Princess Marina of Greece, duchess of Kent, here photographed by Horst (American, born 1906), was one of the most glamorous and least stuffy members of the English royal family. At a coming-out party in the 1950s, she took off her heavy diamond tiara and handed it to the bandleader, who placed it on top of the piano for safekeeping while she danced.

1-38. One night in 1931 after Loelia Ponsonby's marriage to the duke of Westminster, they went dancing at the Embassy, London's famous nightclub. En route, the duke fished from his pocket a gold pin set with a pair of enormous diamonds, saying, "You'd better have these. Put them on." A friend who saw them that night wondered why Loelia was wearing chunks of glass pinned to her dress. In fact, they were the famous Arcot diamonds, later used as the central stones in this tiara.

"This then is a ball. This is life, what we have been waiting for all these years. . . . But, alas, so utterly different from what one had imagined and expected; it must be admitted, not a good dream. The men so small and ugly, the women so frowsty, their clothes so messy and their faces so red, the oil-stoves so smelly, and not really very warm, but, above all, the men, either so old or so ugly. And when they ask one to dance, . . . it is not at all like floating away into a delicious cloud, pressed by a manly arm to a manly bosom, but stumble, stumble, kick, kick."

—Nancy Mitford,
The Pursuit of Love

to the duchess of Westminster. "Of course I went to the Embassy whenever I got the chance; only an angel could have stayed away." The clientele was as top-notch as the music and the food; the four corner tables were usually reserved for the Prince of Wales, the Mountbattens, the duke of Westminster, and ex-King Alfonso of Spain. As Margaret, duchess of Argyll, put it in her autobiography, *Forget Not,* "Everybody in the room knew everybody. The women all wore their best dresses, the men were in white ties—at least, until the Prince of Wales introduced the fashion of wearing the dinner jacket in restaurants."

The Prince of Wales set social fashions as well. He and his "great friend" of the moment, Mrs. Dudley Ward, used to practice dancing together in the mornings at the Café de Paris, another of London's famous nightclubs. In fact, he once kept a band playing steadily for an hour and a half while doing the one-step and the Charleston with Mrs. Ward.

The new steps—and there were constantly new steps—required practice. Dances went in and out of fashion quickly, and demonstrating incompetence was endlessly shaming. In an issue of the English *Woman's Supplement,* readers were warned that "the uninitiated onlooker should not be lured onto the floor by the apparent simplicity of this season's dances. Only study and practice can enable dancers to assume the fashionable look of care-free aimlessness. . . ." Similarly, in 1920, the *Gazette de Bon Genre* gave some pointers: "Do not, Madame, while dancing, twine your left arm around your partner's neck, no matter how much pleasure you think— no doubt correctly—this will give him." Instead, the lady's hand should rest with the little finger on the center seam of her partner's jacket. And "it is permitted to add *jazz* to the fox-trot; abso-

lutely forbidden, on the other hand, is the *shimmy,* with its suggestive trembling, the whites of the eyes showing, the mouth all screwed up." The *Gazette de Bon Genre* wanted its ladies to remain ladylike.

The Charleston made this difficult, with its kicks and shuffles and very short skirts. It did not appear until the mid-twenties, and was met —like the waltz and the turkey trot and the tango before it—with outcries. The vicar of St. Aidan's, a church in Bristol, England, stated publicly that "any lover of the beautiful will die rather than be associated with the Charleston. It is neurotic! It is rotten! It stinks! Phew, open the windows!"

Brave New World

Most people objected because they thought the Charleston would usher in social chaos again, as the waltz and the turkey trot had been expected to do. Social chaos, however, had made a firm landing with the war and was well entrenched. A world that could clasp Elsa Maxwell to its bosom, and a world in which girls from good families took chloroform as a recreational drug, could hardly resist the advent of washed, brushed, and monied parvenus.

Witness the career of Laura Corrigan, a former telephone operator from Cleveland, Ohio, who arrived in London in 1922 and rented a house from Mrs. George Keppel, Edward VII's mistress. Rumor had it that she had requested Mrs. Keppel's guest list along with the lease. Mr. Corrigan, who took no part in his wife's social climbing, stayed in the United States and made lots of money, which Mrs. Corrigan used in the

1-39. This is a photograph by Cecil Beaton (British, 1904–80) of the woman who never became queen, to her great disappointment, and to the dismay of the American colony in London, which had bet on Mrs. Simpson's ultimate success. When the king abdicated, Lady Cunard stormed, "How *could* he do this to me!" His wife, as duchess of Windsor, led a fashionable life instead of a royal one.

most blatant way to get the guests she wanted. She would bring bands and cabaret acts over from the Continent for a night, and her parties often featured a tombola with elaborate prizes such as gold sock-suspenders marked with coronets. The coronets, it turned out, were always appropriate because the tombola was fixed; the highest-ranking guests always won.

Mrs. Corrigan was a fairly benign manifestation of the new age. More threatening was the reckless behavior of the young people; they organized bottle parties and scavenger hunts where they tore around in cars all night. The phenomenon of "crashing" was also new, and highly unwelcome. In 1928, Lady Ellesmere gave a very formal ball at Bridgwater House, where guests danced in the huge gallery beneath paintings by Raphael, Tintoretto, and Titian. The next day, the hostess publicly announced that several hundred uninvited guests had attended the ball, among them the daughter of the earl of Ancaster and Cecil Beaton's sister Baba. Many of the parties given before the stockmarket crash were so huge that the hostess could not keep track of all the guests. Occasionally gate-crashers got too cocky, like, for example, the uniformed ensigns from Newport, Rhode Island's naval base who crashed a

1-40. *Plus ça change*: White-gloved debutantes and their escorts waltz at New York's Debutante Cotillion and Christmas Ball in 1948. However much society has changed, no one doubts that a formal introduction to it, including the pearls and bouquets and white dresses, is still a valid enterprise.

party and were ejected with some difficulty. "Think of my feelings," pleaded one ensign to the hostess, who replied firmly, "Think of mine."

The social mobility in the years between the wars was best represented by the career of Wallis Simpson. The Prince of Wales had tremendous power to bring anyone into fashion, and his fondness for being entertained guaranteed that some of his choices might not be the conventional friends of royalty. He went on a safari, for instance, with Thelma, Lady Furness, the twin sister of Gloria, Mrs. Reginald Vanderbilt. Lady Furness in turn introduced him to a newcomer to London, Mrs. Ernest Simpson. No one had thought much of Mrs. Simpson on her arrival; she wore her hair in ugly knobs over her ears and did not seem terribly attractive. But when, in an ill-judged moment of confidence, Lady Furness instructed Mrs. Simpson to "look after the little man" while she was away, Mrs. Simpson did just that.

It was a moment of unusual brilliance in London for Americans. As the prince and Mrs. Simpson danced discreetly at the Embassy Club with groups of friends, or gave weekend parties at Fort Belvedere, California-born Lady Cunard fantasized about being Mistress of the Robes

1-41. Charles de Beistigui's costume ball at the Palazzo Labia in Venice was a landmark party of the 1950s. The guests' costumes even managed to compete with the frescoes by Giovanni Battista Tiepolo. In this photograph by Cecil Beaton, Daisy Fellowes is "America" in leopard print.

when her friend became queen. Chips Channon, a Chicagoan who had become a British citizen, married a Guinness, and successfully run for Parliament, had his greatest moment when Edward VIII dined at his house in Belgrave Square. These Americans took the abdication hard; Lady Cunard was supposed to have said, "How *could* he do this to me?"

Dancing for Dollars

However much Edward might have let down his partisans in London in the 1930s, he and his duchess went on to bestow a great deal of cachet on social events for the next thirty-odd years, to the extent that their absence could diminish a party's luster. Charles de Beistigui, for instance, gave the fête of the decade in 1951. It was a housewarming for his Palazzo Labia in Venice, bought for $500,000 and refurbished for another $750,000. Some fifteen hundred guests, many of whom were more accustomed to postwar austerity than to frank opulence, arrived at the palazzo by gondola and barge, dressed in costumes from 1743. (Shortly after the invitations were issued, they became available on the black market for five hundred dollars apiece in Paris and Rome.) There were tableaux vivants, acrobats, a ballet, and two bands, not to mention the Tiepolo frescoes in the grand salon. The host changed his clothes six times during the evening, though he stuck to his original shoes with sixteen-inch platforms; he was only five feet six inches tall, and perhaps did not want to be overlooked in the melee. The Aga Khan as an eighteenth-century noble in a wheelchair, Gene Tierney in a peasant dress she had rented for fourteen dollars and Barbara Hutton in one she had had made for several thousands, Lady Diana Cooper in silver fabric and pearls, nobles from all over Europe graced Beistigui's ball. But the duke and duchess of Windsor were not there, and in the scant paragraph of coverage it gave the party, the New York *Times* took care to point that out.

They were fixtures, however, at the balls for the international set and were enormously sought after for the classic social events of the 1950s, the charity balls. At a ball for the benefit of abandoned children in 1950, the courtyard of the Hôtel Lambert on the Île Saint Louis was covered with a dance floor, the windows were

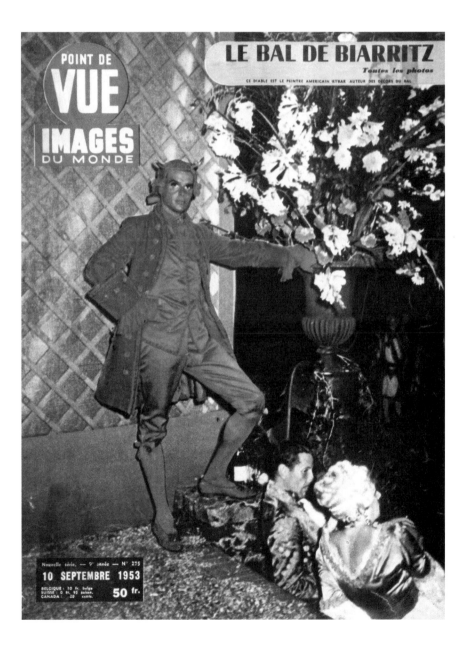

1-42. The de Cuevas ball in Biarritz in 1953 got even more press coverage than Beistigui's ball; here the American painter Valerian Rybar is an eighteenth-century devil complete with horns and red skin, a very literal interpretation.

turned into little imitation opera "boxes," and the duke and duchess gave of their luster. At New York's famous April in Paris Ball in 1957, the duke and duchess outshone Marilyn Monroe and French actor Gérard Philippe, the young Senator and Mrs. Kennedy, and lovely Mrs. Winston Guest. They were even persuaded (somehow) to attend New York's Debutante Cotillion and Christmas Ball, where one young deb asked the duke to dance. He said he had forgotten how to fox-trot.

Of course the Windsors attended only a fraction of the charity balls that filled the fifties, for the benefit of the Red Cross or the Boys' Club or the British RSPCA or hearts or lungs or poverty-stricken White Russians. Night after night, ladies would step into their bouffant dresses and their husbands would clasp their necklaces and off they would go. They would sit at tables of eight or ten in a huge ballroom. They would dine, drink, and dance. There would be people there who were more important than they were, whom they would try to glimpse. Bright lights, music, silks and satins, brocade shoes, flirting, and small talk filled the evening.

Though there were no wigs and the men did not wear makeup and the music was very different, Horace Walpole would certainly have recognized the event. But Walpole would have been shocked at certain aspects of the way this new society enjoyed itself. Actors and actresses and men who had begun their careers as mail-boys mingled with men and women bearing titles that Walpole had known. At a charity ball, everyone had paid to be there or someone had paid for him; and if one had only to pay to be at such a ball, wasn't it possible that *anyone* could go? If money, rather than breeding or friendship with the host, determined entrance to soci-ety's grandest occasions, then it was clear that society's world had been completely transformed since the eighteenth century.

Twist and Shout

In October of 1961, society received another shock. In New York City, at a slightly seedy nightclub known as the Peppermint Lounge, a new dance sprang up. It was called the twist. It was easy to do; the twisting of the hips and the ankles required little in the way of practice or skill. A great deal of improvisation seemed permissible. The motions could be construed as obscene, but the truly shocking thing was that partners danced apart. The man could be in one corner twisting away, looking like a corkscrew trying to wedge its way into a cork, while over in another corner the woman could look as though she were trying to remove chewing gum from her shoe. And they would be dancing together! To the ears of the fifties, the music was cacophony.

The twist was instantly fashionable. The dance hall Roseland banned it within weeks of its emergence. In Paris it caught on very fast. The White House issued a formal denial that anyone had danced the twist at a party in November. It was as bad as the Charleston, or the turkey trot, or the waltz, and like those earlier dances it would lead to the decay of society. Society absorbed the twist, as it has absorbed other dances, newcomers, and scandalous modes of behavior for two hundred years. Society continues to dance.

1-43. Countess Bismarck was the daughter of a horse trainer who married her father's boss before she was twenty. Two divorces later she became Mrs. Harrison Williams, a fixture on the best-dressed list. Her apotheosis as countess Bismarck occurred when she married, in 1955, the interior decorator grandson of the Iron Prince.

Dancing Lessons

1. *Right: The Dance* by Martin Engelbrecht (German, 1684–1756), an engraving of about 1730, shows gentlemen learning to dance the minuet.

2. *Below: The Comforts of Bath: Private Practices Previous to the Ball* by Thomas Rowlandson

3. *Above: The Dancing Lesson,* an engraving after a painting by Emil Adam (German, 1843–after 1885)

4. *Left: The Dancing Lesson* by Jacques-Philippe Lebas (French, 1707–1783)

5. *Right*: Mr. Owen's Institution, New Lanark, an aquatint of 1825 by George Hunt (British, active 19th century), shows children learning basic cotillion and contredanse forms.

6. *Left: The Dancing Lesson: Part 2, The Minuet*, a colored etching of 1835 by George Cruikshank (British, 1792–1878)

7. *Below:* Engraving from *La Gazette de Bon Ton*, 1920

Stages of the Ball

1. *Right: Winter* by Alfred Stevens
   (American, 1828–1906)

2. *Below:* Dior ball gown photographed in Paris in 1950 by
   Louise Dahl-Wolfe (American,
   born 1895)

3. *Below:* "Les Préparatifs du Bal"
   from *Le Bon Genre*, 1801

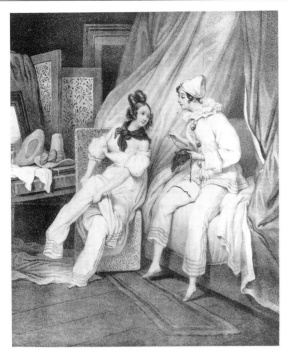

4. *Left: Les Apprêts du Bal,* an engraving after Paul Gavarni (French, 1804–66)

5. *Below:* Dorian Leigh wearing an evening dress by Piguet in Helena Rubinstein's Paris apartment, photographed in 1949 by Richard Avedon (American, born 1923)

6. *Above: The Allegory Dance* by Hans
   Lefler (German, 1828–1906)

7. *Right:* Engraving from *Fashions of
   London,* 1798

8. *Above: Duel After the Masquerade* by
   Jean-Léon Gérôme (French,
   1824–1904)

9. *Right: After the Ball* by Alfred Stevens

The Evolution of Social Dancing

by Don McDonagh

In 1914, as the world was edging toward war, Irene Castle made news of another kind: She had her appendix out. With her appendectomy, the growing controversy over the morality of the dances inspired by ragtime took another turn, and, as she wrote in her autobiography, *Castles in the Air*, "the doctors got into the act. Half of them tried to prove that dancing had damaged my appendix and caused the attack. The rest of them stoutly defended both my appendix and my dancing. Dancing was good clean exercise, they said, and definitely therapeutic." Since the Renaissance, social dancing has sparked just such a combination of controversy and delight and has been both roundly praised and soundly condemned.

Before the Renaissance, dancing had for the most part existed as a somewhat unrefined activity engaged in by the peasantry, but in the fifteenth century, as the world felt the first stirrings of modern secularism, dance was elevated to a new status. Those in power saw the dance as an instructional discipline for their dependent nobility and as a means of self-aggrandizement.

The forms of court dance that first emerged expressed socially approved behavior between men and women, and as these relations changed so did the dances. To insure conformity to a strict standard, dancing masters became fixtures in noble courts. These teachers, ordinarily not of noble birth themselves, had shown proficiency in personal performance, and they regularly reworked vigorous peasant dancing into socially restrained forms with clear measures and patterns.

The dances were taught to everyone who had social ambitions, and once perfected they became marks of a gentleman's accomplishments, on a par with fancy riding (*dressage*) and fencing (*escrime*). One of the qualities that distinguished

2-1. Basse danze, or low dances, were named for the gliding movements close to the floor that were their most prominent feature. Dancing was clearly an affair of probity rather than personal enjoyment, judging from the watchful eye of the local nobleman looking on from his throne.

2-2. *Left:* Hops, leaps, and kicks were excitingly incorporated into "high dances" performed to lively tempos. As was customary in the fifteenth century, men were allowed far greater leeway than women in such activity.

2-3. *Below:* The ball held in 1581 for the marriage of Margaret of Lorraine to the duc de Joyeuse was the most expensive event of its kind that had ever been staged. It was Henri III's farewell to a young man to whom he had been closely attached for some years, and in recognition of the occasion's solemnity, the courtiers dance a stately pavane, which not only reflects their dignity but also shows their lavish clothing to its greatest advantage.

court dances from the peasant versions was their international character. Folk dances remained imbedded in the society that had given them birth, whereas court dances quite readily jumped national borders. The Italian basse danze, or low dances, constitute the earliest group about which we have any detailed information. They featured walking or gliding steps rather than the leaps, hops, and kicks of folk dances. They could be found in England, France, Germany, and Spain, where local modifications were introduced quite comfortably by dancers who were not Italian.

In our own time, the classic ballroom dances display the same international character: the waltz (Austria/Germany), fox-trot (United States), tango (Argentina), rumba (Cuba). Today's dances also follow the same developmental pattern as earlier dances, appearing first among those on the lowest rungs of the social ladder and gradually gaining general acceptance. During the process the rough edges are knocked off, dance teachers standardize the steps and patterns, and the resultant work is

2-4. Queen Elizabeth I of England loved to dance, the more vigorously the better. Here, the earl of Leicester lifts her in the air doing the volta, a curious dance that relied heavily on the strength of the costume as well as the male partner.

"Many, many with whom I have conversed, tell me that at no time for the last sixty or seventy years was frivolity, the love of pleasure, self-indulgence, and idleness (producing ignorance) carried to such excess as now in the Higher Classes, and that it resembles the time before the first French Revolution; and I must— alas!—admit that this is true."

—Queen Victoria, in a letter to the Prince of Wales

Queen Elizabeth dancing *lavolta* with the Earl of Leicester.

included in the repertory of dances offered for instruction. Few dances actually become classics; most are simply novelties that enjoy a brief turn on the dance floor.

The attrition rate was equally high among court dances, although little is known about the specific forms or even names of pre-fifteenth-century dances. With the advent of the printed word during the Renaissance, dance manuals were printed and circulated, and surviving examples provide the names and descriptions of the dances, including at times illustrations and even the music used to accompany them.

The dancing masters of northern Italy achieved new status through their association with such leading families as the Medici of Florence, Sforza of Milan, Farnese of Parma, Gonzaga of Mantua, and d'Este of Ferrara. Domenico da Piacenza, later known as Domenico of Ferrara for his service there, is generally acknowledged as the most distinguished dancing master of the first half of the fifteenth century. In 1416 he published, in Latin, a dance manual *De Arte Saltandi et Choreas Ducendi*, subtitled in the vernacular *De la Arte di Ballare et Danzare*. Two of his pupils, Guglielmo Ebreo (William the Jew) of Pesaro and Antonio Cornazano of Piacenza, published manuals of their own in Italian in which they developed the principles laid down by Domenico.

These manuals reveal certain preoccupations that have persisted from the earliest days of court dancing to our own day of social dancing. Domenico clearly believed in the civilizing influence of dance, and he distanced himself from those who did not. He tried to dissociate himself from those who would not accept the discipline of dancing and the restraints it imposed. "And nevertheless there have been many who were opposed to this ardent and free mobil-

2-6. The half-turned feet, here clearly demonstrated by the gentleman in fourth position, were essential to the proper performance of all court dances during the seventeenth century. Each step began and ended in one of the five positions.

ity exercised with great subtlety and discernment as being lascivious and wanton. But the author [Domenico] argued against this with righteous zeal, saying that all things are liable to corruption and degeneration if they are employed indiscreetly—that is, with exaggeration. It is moderation that conserves." And addressing the male practitioner directly, he continues, "And note, *galante*, that by the exercise of bodily mobility, avoiding all extravagance, this gentle art, I say, will have within itself a natural beauty and much decorum thereby." With variations, these are themes that dance masters and instructors have repeated in almost every generation. In our own time the late William deRham cautioned little boys in his classes that it was impolite to leave their partners until they "found another partner or got married." He may have exaggerated, but the point was made and remembered.

Domenico set down his thoughts on dancing in the first quarter of the fifteenth century, the era of the basse danse, which were performed everywhere substantially as Domenico described them. Because these serene and gently undulating dances depended on lifting the heels slowly and lowering them quickly, Domenico likened the motion to that of a double-oared gondola cresting and dipping quickly into the trough of the next wave.

He referred to the rhythm as the "queen of measures," unlike others such as the *piva*, a rapid measure used by the peasants (*villani*) for their dances. The stately, deliberate pacing of the basse danse may resemble the motion of the gondola, but it can be traced to the measured gait of the camel. The dances' measure was adapted from camel driver chants, which had entered the mainstream of Moorish music. During the three centuries of near-total Moorish

2-7. The sense of pastoral elegance was part and parcel of aristocratic dancing. Jean-Antoine Watteau (French, 1684–1721) regarded the dance as a metaphor for all earthly pleasures.

domination of the Iberian peninsula, this basic rhythm influenced the Spanish musical tradition. Even today the word *arabesque* ("in the arab manner"), in the vocabulary of classic ballet, an offshoot of court dancing, recognizes a Muslim source. During the twelfth and thirteenth centuries, as Christian Spain recovered much of its northern territory, commercial contacts between Barcelona in Aragon and the ports of northern Italy were steady and substantial. The Aragonese royal family eventually added Naples and Sicily to its suzerainty, and Spanish families such as the Borgias settled in Italy, bringing with them cultural as well as commercial influences. By Domenico's time, basse danze in various forms were firmly established in both Italy and Spain.

Also firmly established were the five basic foot positions that began or ended all of the steps

in the basse danze and subsequent court dances. Unlike the normal parallel positions of the feet, in the dance positions the toes were turned outward to form an angle of 90 degrees so that the legs were seen in half-profile instead of straight on. By the eighteenth century, when professional ballet emerged from amateur court dance, the turnout was established at 180 degrees, showing the legs in full profile.

Dances customarily began with a reverence, or bow, during which the man removed his hat and extended his left leg forward; being closer to the heart, the left leg was considered more gallant. The woman's complementary curtsy and arm movements were more restrained. When the sequence of dance steps was accomplished, the dance ended with a less elaborate reverence. The steps—"singles," "doubles," "continenzas," and so forth—were standardized, and a writer could describe a dance by listing them in proper sequence and indicating the number of repetitions. After a bassa danza, it was customary to perform the saltarello, a court dance of different mood. The Spanish called it *alta danza* (high dance) to emphasize the liveliness that characterized its swaying movement and little jumps.

Throughout the history of social dancing, there have been two basic groups of dances. Low, gliding, and turning steps provide the vocabulary of one group, from the basse danse through the waltz, fox-trot, and twist, while jumps, kicks, and hops characterize the other group, starting with the saltarello and including the polka, Charleston, and lindy hop. The proud, ambitious Renaissance man acquired a thin veneer of manners through the steady application of such formal exercises.

The basse danze persisted for a century and a half, owing their longevity to their adaptability. In southern France in the sixteenth century, one such adaptation was the branle. It took its name from the French verb *branler,* meaning to shake or wag, and was characterized by a swinging, balanced, side-to-side movement, performed with speed and an evenly timed lifting and lowering of the heels. The couples were now linked in horizontal lines, all doing the same step at the same time. Because there were twice as many measures per minute, the group was as lively and vigorous as a unison precision team.

A beautiful walking dance of the time was the pavane, alternatively given Italian or Spanish origins by dance historians. Because the word *pavane* seems rooted in the Spanish *pavo* (peacock), the balance tips in favor of Spain, and certainly, the spirit of the dance seems to convey the sense of peacocks preening. One form of the dance is a processional in which a line of couples, colorfully dressed for a grand occasion, performs such functions as escorting a young bride to church or opening a court ball.

However beautiful it may be, the pavane did not lend itself to many modifications. Dances that introduce a new rhythm are most likely to inspire development. The branle was such a dance, becoming the central developmental form of the sixteenth century. Like the basse danze, it was easily modified, and there were soon sprightly versions that involved kicking steps as well as hops and turns. A particular favorite, named for a province of southern France, was the branle de Poitou, which had small, light, delicate steps and would itself evolve into the minuet.

With the branle, there was a shift to France as the center of the dance world. By the end of the sixteenth century, most of the court dancing masters were French instead of Italian, and a French priest, Jehan Tabourot, had published one of the most respected manuals on court dance and the mores of his time. In 1589, using the anagram pen name Thoinot Arbeau, Tabourot completed his *Orchésographie* ("dance-writing"). He was sixty-nine years old and died the same year. A local publisher in the town of Langres found the manuscript among the vicar's papers and, with the permission of the family, published it posthumously later in that year.

As a thorough Renaissance man Tabourot used the Socratic dialogues as his teaching model and invented a mythical young pupil named Capriol with whom to converse. The name itself is a play on words: a capriole was a specific type of high jump. In response to the young man's "questions," Tabourot describes the

2-8. During the Renaissance dancing masters relied on verbal descriptions, but subsequent teachers continually sought more precise methods of describing specific dances. The floor patterns and step indications of the Beauchamps–Feuillet system were widely used during the seventeenth and eighteenth centuries.

B. II.   *The Conclusion or Presenting of Both Arms.*   P. XII.

K. T. inv.t   Finis.   *Arnold Vanhaecken delin G. King sculpsit.*

2-9. The woman's fan became an essential tool in the ballroom. This fan was also used to display a panoramic view of a ball like those at which it was probably used.

dances he performed as a young man or observed during his long life. As he proceeds, he tosses in witty and perceptive comments about manners and customs of the time.

That a priest in good standing with his church should write a text on this subject is unusual. Perhaps Tabourot's use of a pen name and his failure to publish during his lifetime reflect something of the ambiguous attitude of ecclesiastical authorities toward dancing, for the practice had been alternately condemned and permitted. Tabourot cited scripture as precedent; after all, King David danced before the Ark of the Lord, and weddings and other (unspecified) rites in religious festivals were celebrated with dancing. Exhibiting a peculiarly French testiness, Tabourot lashed out at disapproving reformers by suggesting that they be fed a vile-sounding concoction of goat's-meat pie prepared without bacon.

He further defends dancing on practical grounds as a test of a young man's or woman's health. He even approves of a postdance kiss that draws the couple close enough to ascertain the partner's shapeliness and detect any unhealthy odor like "bad meat." Finally he observes that dance is an essential part of a well-ordered society. He sounds the same themes that Domenico of Ferrara had expressed over a century and a half earlier. Obviously, dancing continued to pose a problem to moral authorities. In addition to descriptions of the older dances and over a dozen branles, Tabourot mentions the allemand (alman), courante (coranto), canary, gavotte, morris dances (morisque), volta (lavolta), and several galliards.

Across the English Channel, the courtiers of Queen Elizabeth I danced vigorously, none more enthusiastically than the monarch herself. It was said that she performed a half dozen or so galliards before breakfast each morning, and in a woodcut she is shown dancing the volta with the earl of Leicester. At the time, this hopping and leaping dance was considered rather daring, for the man placed one hand about his partner's waist, the other on her stomach, and boosted her high in the air with his thigh under her buttocks. (One wonders what the peasant original of this dance was like if this was the toned-down version!) The woman steadied herself by placing her right hand on her partner's shoulder, using her left hand to hold her skirt, as the queen does in this woodcut, and to keep from exposing a knee or even a thigh.

Even the tolerant Tabourot was somewhat dubious about the volta, wondering whether honor and health might not be compromised. His pupil Capriol suggests that such dancing was not proper for gentlefolk but was acceptable when dancing with a strapping hussy. The English court did not mind the dance at all. It was but one of many sprightly dances that was widely performed. Shakespeare mentions the pavane, canary (caneri), passemezzo (passy measures pavyn), courante (coranto), gigue (jig), and, of course, the galliard.

Elizabeth I liked to see her courtiers dance the lively galliard as energetically as possible. One five-step sequence (*cinq pas* became *sink-a-pace* in English) included a final high leap, known as a caper, with both feet leaving the ground. Hence the saying "to cut a caper," which in our time has evolved from its precise original meaning to include all frolicsome leaping and dancing.

During the seventeenth century, the galliard

2-10–12. *Below*: The introduction of liberated touch dancing at the end of the eighteenth century set a new style for the nineteenth in the ballroom. Feet were no longer turned out, and partners embraced in public, much to the horror of traditionalists.

Asking to dance   Leading out   Hands four round   Down the middle   Right and left   Setting

Cross hands   Poussette   Hornpipe   Tête à tête   Fainting   Taking home royal

2-13. This set of instructional pictographs, which starts with a gracious invitation and ends with an exhausted exit, was used to teach a country dance in an eighteenth-century dancing manual.

fell from favor and was replaced by the courante and saraband as the most popular dances at the French court. The courante gained favor as a running-step alternative to the bouncy galliard, and the dignified, processional saraband suited Louis XIII "Le Just" admirably.

With the saraband's somewhat checkered past, the road to court was a long one. The dance is thought to have originated during the twelfth century in Spain, when the country was under Moorish domination. According to legend, it was named by a devil disguised as a woman. Its association with notorious courtesans led to its suppression for a time by King Philip II of Spain. A disapproving commentator, Pedro Marianna, condemned the saraband as lascivious, ugly, and a disgrace to Spain, but by the turn of the seventeenth century, the dance was enough like a pavane to be performed without scandal and to become quite fashionable.

For two centuries—from 1500 to 1700—while profound changes had occurred in dance, there were corresponding changes in music. The dancing masters required precise beats and measures in order to standardize and record their dances. Most dancing masters were also adept at playing an instrument and arranging folk airs in suitable dance form. The earlier dances were accompanied at times by songs or by a single wind or stringed instrument and a drum. Later, the numbers and variety of instruments grew. Professional composers seeking employment at various courts developed great skill at arranging

and creating original melodies in the requisite dance rhythms. They also developed the musical suite to add balance and variety to court dancing. Originally these suites included the allemand, courante, saraband, and gigue. Later, five- and six-part suites, including the minuet, were developed. These independent units eventually formed an integrated sonata, freed to pursue an exclusively musical logic without reference to dance or verbal text.

France continued to be the arbiter of taste for court dancing in Europe until the end of the eighteenth century. No matter where a new dance might originate, it received its final form and polish in France. The courante unfortunately was polished to the point of dullness under the eye of King Louis XIII. It became slow and gravely elegant by the time it crossed to England and was of little interest. After attending a court ball in 1666, Samuel Pepys noted in his diary "that the corants [sic] grew tiresome." And well they might, for there were three times as many courantes as other dances that evening.

The French dancing masters, as an alternative to the tedious courante, offered the delightfully accommodating branle de Poitou, adding a new wrinkle to it. The light and delicate *pas menu* (little step) was retained, but the group formation was broken into couples. The first couple led the others in an S- or Z-pattern across the ballroom floor. Later, circular, question-mark-shaped, and other patterns were developed. While the pattern and dance steps were firmly set, the dancers were allowed some discretion as to the sequence of steps and number of repeats each time they performed the new minuet. (Originally the term *menuet* was used to describe any dance of small steps.)

As Domenico in the fifteenth century designated the basse danze the "queen of measures," the French court referred to the minuet as the "queen of dances." It was the favorite of Louis XIV, who was reputed to have taken daily dancing lessons. His instructor, Pierre Beauchamps, was subsequently appointed director of the Académie Royale de Danse, Europe's first professional ballet school. Bows and curtsies decorated the small, dainty steps of the minuet throughout the dance, not just at the beginning and end, with more and more refinements added to the positions of the arms and hands, until the minuet was the most elaborate and artificial form of court dancing ever seen.

During Louis XIV's long and successful reign, all things tasteful and artistically refined were epitomized by the splendor of the French court. Versailles not only was the center of France, it was the center of Europe. When the monarch and his courtiers danced, they did so with awareness of their own importance and elegant dignity. At the beginning of the century, heels were added to the flat, soft leather dancing shoes. Buckles, bows, and ever higher heels, in evidence in the Sun King's court, were perfect for the small, measured steps of the minuet. Soon all Europe followed suit.

The death of Louis XIV at the beginning of the eighteenth century represented the end of France's most glorious hour, but the minuet persisted. It was still danced at court, but Louis XV was not so self-consciously dignified and sought lighter diversion in the frisky contredanse (country dance) imported from England. The couples faced one another in rows or formed circles, performing such variations as the quadrille and cotillion, which shared the same lively, light-hearted character as the contredanse.

The artificial gaiety of nobles playing at peasant dances increased in Louis XVI's court, although the minuet was still an important ritual at court balls. The political power of the monarchy, however, had been seriously undermined, and revolutionaries assumed direction of the government. At the age of thirty-eight Louis XVI was beheaded. With him died the system of absolute monarchy in France and the style of court dancing as it had been known since the early Renaissance.

"Neither the men nor the women dance well; all stretch out and lengthen their arms in a way far from agreeable."
—*Claude Blanchard, eighteenth-century visitor to the United States*

2-14, 15. The quadrille was a square dance performed in five different tempos. Hundreds of variations were developed in the nineteenth century to add interest to the basic pattern.

L'ÉTÉ.

L'ANGLAISE.

2-16. *Right:* Elegance and energy were what made the waltz the dominant dance of the nineteenth century. Johann Strauss, Jr., who filled Europe's ballrooms with his lilting melodies, conducted with his violin bow when he was not actually playing with the orchestra.

2-18. *Opposite:* The North German galop appeared, here depicted by Paul Gavarni, after the waltz had emerged in South Germany and Austria. Dancers found it a delightful change of pace and happily incorporated it into their quadrilles.

2-17. *Below:* Even in a vigorous waltz, gentlemen were able to keep their top hats securely in place.

The noble style of dancing persisted in ballet which, in the hands of professionals, would follow its own spectacular development. In the countryside, folk dancing continued much as it had in the past. Social dancing as we know it today began with the newly emerging middle class of the nineteenth century. Shreds of manners and old ways hung on, as did the minuet in various European courts and in parts of the young United States. However, in the rough-and-ready atmosphere of the New World, court dancing with its reverences and open couple formations was quickly transformed into country dancing. The caller replaced the dancing master, and the brief opening command "Honor your partner" became a pale reflection of the hat-sweeping reverence of earlier days.

The formality and ritual of European dance were changing as well. In the German and Austrian countryside, peasants had been doing a centuries-old closed-couple turning dance called the ländler. It would have been shocking for people of breeding to embrace so openly in public, but the peasants had their own customs. However, this particular dance appealed to the changing spirit of the times as Romanticism captured the European imagination. By the late eighteenth century, a suitably polished ländler, renamed the waltz, appeared in Viennese ballrooms.

Renaissance court dancing had been a formal and dignified exercise of manners between men and women. Women were considered maidenly figures to be approached with courtesy, escorted around the dance floor with dignity, and not held closely in public. Romance was a luxury the nobility could scarcely afford in troubled times when arranged marriages were one means of achieving political ends. While the more playful dances of the seventeenth and eighteenth centuries expressed a slightly more relaxed attitude, relationships between the sexes were still quite formal. Group dancing at arm's length, carefully watched by the arbiters of manners, was the norm.

The waltz completely repudiated four centuries of such dance practice. It was denounced, deplored, and banned at times for its "immorality" but was irresistible to the independent-minded and the newly powerful middle class. Joseph Lanner, Johann Strauss, and Johann Strauss, Jr., wrote waltz music of such captivating charm that it was played everywhere. The waltz became the dance of the nineteenth century. Couples whirled around the dance floor in private homes and public ballrooms. "Touch" dancing had arrived in polite society; it was

2-19. The large subscription halls that replaced private drawing rooms in nineteenth-century Europe were exceptionally popular. Competition for membership in the more exclusive halls was keen, because members did all the most recent dances, such as the polka seen here.

engaged in by kings and queens, lords and ladies, and members of the bourgeoisie.

The waltz so dominated the era that on a typical program of twenty-four dances, nineteen would be waltzes. Gone were the turned-out toes in favor of the natural parallel position of the feet. Gone were the bows and arm's-length "truce" position, and gone was the rigid control of set forms and dance formations. Where logic and rules had dominated, now the power of individual emotions determined behavior. Those emotions propelled men and women into each other's arms in public, with the closed couple constituting a private world in a public place.

The triumph of the waltz was not immediate, and modified court dances such as the quadrille, cotillion, and lancers were widely performed in more conservative circles. As in earlier dances, groups of couples, usually four, alternately exchanged places and followed set patterns of movement. Allen Dodworth, the most influential teacher in New York, was at pains to emphasize that a dancing school was "not a place of amusement" but that it instilled social and personal standards. His dance manual emphasized deportment as much as the proper execution of the steps of his favored cotillion. Despite such opposition, another closed-couple dance, the

polka, appeared around the middle of the nineteenth century and was taken up enthusiastically. It combined the turning of the waltz with a hop step. By the end of the century, the closed-couple dance had won the day without question.

Up to this time the United States had passively followed Europe's lead, but the vigorous march rhythm of John Philip Sousa's compositions inspired an American innovation, the two-step. A simple dance with an exciting beat, it alternated between an open and closed position and became the most popular dance of the Gay Nineties on both sides of the Atlantic.

Dance responded to new musical rhythms, and when ragtime was heard beyond the "sporting district" of New Orleans where it had originated, it set off a dance craze in the United States and Europe in the years before World War I. Nothing like the turkey trot (condemned by the Vatican, among others), bunny hug, grizzly bear, kangaroo hop, snake, and camel walk had been seen in polite society before. With names more appropriate to a zoo than a ballroom, the new dances were athletic and bouncy, and the partners were closer than ever before. It had taken four centuries for partners to come within an arm's length, but the distance was diminish-

2-20–22. Choreographic notation has changed with almost every generation and has often been so complex that only experts can read it. The 1713 notation system of Feuillet and Desaix, *below right*, looks almost hieroglyphic, and the careful eighteenth-century diagram of the figures of a contredanse, *below*, looks more like a strategic plan than a stately court dance. But the 1945 footstep patterns of Veloz and Yolanda, *right*, are completely legible to our twentieth-century eyes.

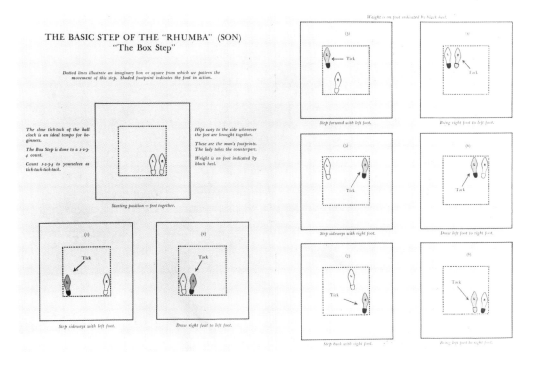

THE BASIC STEP OF THE "RHUMBA" (SON)
"The Box Step"

Dotted lines illustrate an imaginary box or square from which we pattern the movement of this step. Shaded footprint indicates the foot in action.

The slow tick-tack of the hall clock is an ideal tempo for beginners.

The Box Step is done to a 1-2-3-4 count.

Count 1-2-3-4 to yourselves as tick-tack-tick-tack.

Hips sway to the side whenever the feet are brought together.

These are the man's footprints. The lady takes the counterpart.

Weight is on foot indicated by black heel.

Starting position — feet together.

(1) Step sideways with left foot.

(2) Draw right foot to left foot.

(3) Step forward with left foot.

(4) Bring right foot to left foot.

(5) Step sideways with right foot.

(6) Draw left foot to right foot.

(7) Step back with right foot.

(8) Bring left foot to right foot.

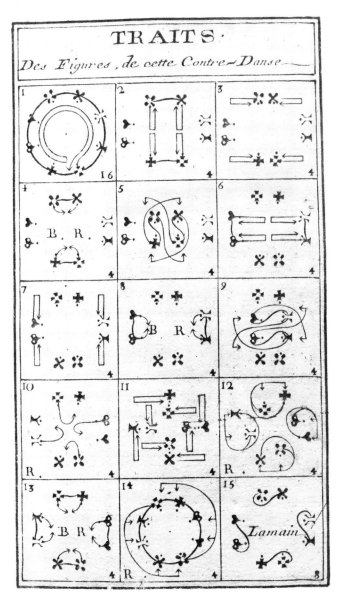

TRAITS.
Des Figures, de cette Contre-Danse

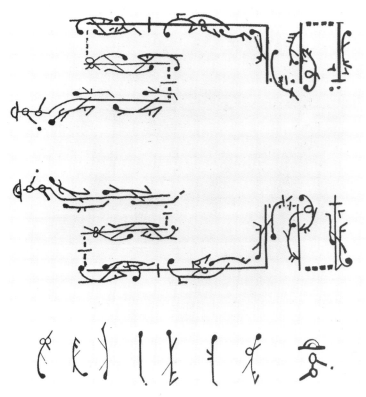

"Why, there are only about four hundred people in fashionable New York Society. If you go outside that number you strike people who are either not at ease in a ballroom or else make other people not at ease."

—Ward McAllister, in the
New York Tribune, 25 March 1888.

2-23. The delightful woodcut below of 1899 by Pierre Vidal (French, 1849–1929) shows a number of working-class couples kicking up their heels over the rooftops of Paris. One woman performs the notorious show dance, the can-can, which began as a social dance akin to the quadrille but became so high-spirited in music halls and allowed such profligate displays of frilly undergarments that it was banned for a time.

2-24. *Opposite:* Straightforward enthusiasm was the primary requirement for patrons of the less exclusive cabarets, which were frequented by pleasure-seeking Parisians of the late nineteenth century. Henri de Toulouse-Lautrec (French, 1864–1901) perfectly captures their dynamic earthiness in his *Quadrille at the Moulin Rouge*, 1892.

"The classes below, from which their children are slowly bringing recruits, are gradually imposing changes on the etiquette of the classes above; changes which the elders struggle against in vain."
—Vogue, *1 July 1922*

ing at an accelerated pace, and in the menagerie dances the couples danced cheek to cheek! They hung on each other's shoulders and necks as they swayed and jogged along.

People struggled to keep pace with each "latest" dance, learning the steps from such innovators as Irene and Vernon Castle, the best-known exhibition dancers of their time. Suave and elegant, the Castles smoothed out the more grotesque gyrations of the new dances. People came to see their demonstrations at popular late afternoon *thés dansants* (tea dances) in hotel ballrooms. When the Castles had finished the last step of the latest dance, couples swarmed to the floor to try the new steps. They loved the Castle Walk and a politely modified version of the notorious tango, which the Castles had encountered in Paris.

From the same era, that perennial favorite the fox-trot is one of the few classic ballroom standards that can be traced to a specific choreographer. Harry Fox and Yanszieka Deutsch, one of the Dolly Sisters, formed an exhibition ballroom dance team that appeared in the 1913 edition of the Ziegfeld *Follies*. Their staged dance routine was adapted and slowed down by

teacher Oscar Duryea, eventually becoming the most popular ballroom dance of the twentieth century.

World War I had a profound effect on the structure of society. The role of women was changing. During the war, they had served in desk jobs in the army to free men for front-line duty. Universal suffrage, full property rights, and recent forays into the business world expanded women's horizons far beyond the home. Their new freedom was reflected in clothing that was less cumbersome than the turn-of-the-century waist cinchers, voluminous dresses, and tiny hats atop elaborate hairdos. And as ragtime

for alcohol that drove some people to foreign shores for wet vacations. Nearby Havana was a favorite watering hole, and there many tourists discovered a taste for the rumba along with their rum, just as earlier vacationers had learned to love the tango in Paris. These two dances were the first of a host of Latin rhythms that would appear in ballrooms around the world. Tango songs recounted tales of sadness, disappointment, and despair. The dancers acted as if locked in a stylized duel, at one moment thrusting and withdrawing legs, at another stalking beside one another in a restless prowl. The dance, as presented by the dance team of Valen-

2-25. *Above*: The close embrace of the waltz was further exaggerated in such menagerie dances of the pre–World War I era as the grizzly bear and the bunny hug. Here a couple does the turkey trot, adopting an attitude of proximity that looks more awkward than scandalously licentious.

2-26. *Right:* Irene and Vernon Castle embodied the style and restraint that ragtime dances threatened to drive from the ballroom floor. They set the standard for decorum until Vernon was killed in 1918 when his airplane crashed during a military training flight.

gave way to the rhythms of jazz, libertine new dances epitomized by the Charleston also reflected the spirit of the twenties. Tubular dresses, high hemlines, and bare arms gave women an adolescent, athletic look. They tossed their newly "bobbed" hair and liberated limbs in high kicks, swung their knees open and closed, and crossed arms back and forth. The Charleston was a naughty-and-nice dance that exactly suited the time and inspired other wild dances—the black bottom and varsity drag, for example.

Prohibition also had an effect on the life style of the twenties. It seemed to stimulate a thirst

tino and Rambova (Rodolpho Guglielmi and his wife, Winifred Shaughnessy), smoldered with passionate glances and parted lips.

The decade and its freewheeling life style came to an end with the 1929 stock-market crash in New York. The country was plunged into a financial depression that lasted until the start of World War II. Moviegoers found escape from everyday cares in the Hollywood musicals, a form played to perfection by Fred Astaire and Ginger Rogers, who became the most imitated ballroom couple of the time. Outside the movie theaters, the public found diversion in the swing arrangements of the big bands. Like ragtime and jazz, swing inspired a new dance, the lindy hop, named after Charles Lindbergh and his solo "hop" across the Atlantic in 1927. As first performed in the Savoy Ballroom in New York's Harlem, the dance featured hopping steps, syncopated swings, and lots of turns under the arms as partners moved away from and toward one another.

Even more energetic were the aerial moves of boogie-woogie, a jitterbug variant of the lindy, which flourished in the forties as the world fought another war. The high-flying excesses of boogie-woogie were beyond most ballroom dancers, however, and the samba, which had an intriguing Latin rhythm and bouncy upper-body and arm movements, offered a popular alternative. Thousands of fairgoers saw the samba performed at the Brazilian Pavilion of the 1939–40 New York World's Fair; the dance also received a tremendous boost from Carmen Miranda's appearances in Hollywood musicals.

2-27. *Above:* No dance demonstrated more accurately the verve of the "roaring twenties" than the Charleston. Its sassy athleticism was a far cry from the dances Mother used to do, and the hemline it required was a great deal shorter than hers.

2-28. *Left:* The tango was the first Latin-rhythm dance to gain international acceptance. It was transported from Buenos Aires to Paris before World War I and spread rapidly. This dramatic couple is performing the corte step of the *tango del amor* aboard the S.S. *France*.

The infusion of Latin dances continued in the fifties with the mambo, merengue, and cha-cha, which were popular with adults. However, in the post-World War II years a new youth culture was emerging. They performed entirely different dances that emphasized casual unconcern. The stroll was a group dance resembling a Virginia reel but performed with walking deliberateness. "Touch" dancing was still the norm, but in a slow dance such as the creep it was almost a fossilized shuffling. Rock-and-roll records began to make their appearance on the best-seller charts, and as the decade progressed Elvis Presley appeared on the charts alongside Frank Sinatra, Perry Como, and Tommy Dorsey. Elvis rode to the top on a new wave of consumerism—a children's crusade of consumption. Television reflected the polarity of old and new. Arthur Murray's "Dance Party" featured the ballroom standards while Dick Clark's "American Bandstand" showcased rock and roll and the new teenagers' dances. The choice was clear.

In the early sixties, "American Bandstand" introduced a new performer and a dance that radically changed the nature of social dancing. When Chubby Checker (Ernest Evans) appeared on the show, singing and doing the twist, it was the beginning of the end for "touch" dancing. The era that began in the late eighteenth century with the waltz was over. Predictably, social commentators denounced the twist as fervently as their predecessors had lambasted the waltz or the fox-trot. Dancers swiveled their hips, pumped their hands, shifting weight from foot to foot as if they were snuffing out a cigarette. The twist may have started in Philadelphia on a teenagers' dance program, but it soon broke the social barrier at a nightclub off Times Square in New York. The Peppermint Lounge's normally seedy clientele was elbowed aside as socialites and celebrities crowded in to hear Joey Dee and the Starlighters sing "The Peppermint Twist" and to do the new dance themselves. The twist became the rage, and like earlier dances it spawned a variety of spinoffs—the frug, swim, monkey, jerk, mashed potato, and others too numerous to name.

As a new generation of dances held sway, the old ballroom in its many guises gave way to another phenomenon of the sixties—the discothèque, or simply the disco. Started in Paris, the disco was a nightclub that replaced live with recorded music. Most discos were crowded, cavelike places that vibrated with music and elaborate shows of strobes and colored lights.

2-29. *Opposite:* Fred Astaire and Ginger Rogers epitomized social dancing during the 1930s. Commenting on their successful partnership, Katharine Hepburn once quipped, "She gives him sex and he gives her class."

2-30. After the appearance of the lindy hop, inspired by Charles A. Lindbergh's flight in 1929, jazz dancing became even more exhibitionist during the 1940s, as shown in this wood engraving by Lou Barlow (American, born 1906).

2-32. *Opposite:* The more daring
maneuvers of jazz dancing
ultimately appeared on more repu-
table dance floors. The expression
of the man on the right, however,
proves that their practice was not
without criticism in the 1940s.

2-31. *Below:* The Peppermint
Lounge in New York introduced
the "no-touch" style of dancing to
eager adult participants in the early
1960s. The shoelessness and
tielessness of the male dancer was
shocking to members of the press
at the time.

From the East Village to Park Avenue, New York's discos, like the twist, were the new rage. "Do your own thing" was the battle cry of the decade, and disco dancing accompanied art openings, weddings, and every occasion in between. The dances came and went so fast that dance teachers barely had time to ready them for instruction. Deportment had definitely taken a back seat to the sheer pleasure of rhythmic movement.

Social dancing is a continually evolving form reflecting ever-changing relations between the sexes. To a great extent it has reflected the changing role of woman: from political chattel to independent individual. Dancing does not initiate change but reflects it. From the beginning, it has been pursued both as a civilizing activity and as a recreational exercise, facets that have been alternately praised and condemned over the centuries. Dance has moved from the Renaissance court to public assembly halls, hotel ballrooms, clubs, discos, and private homes, each move representing a political/economic change in society. Like these changing venues, the form of the dance will depend on the spirit of the time. Measured drilling under the watchful eye of a sixteenth-century monarch represented its most supervised state, while swaying and shuffling in the anonymous mass of a disco floor is at the opposite pole. Whatever the shape of the dance or the space for dancing, the dance itself will continue as men and women will always dance, moving together, toward each other, to the beat of the music. The wag who said dancing was the "vertical expression of a horizontal thought" told part of the truth about social dancing. Its existence is an expression of sexual relations, but the variety of its forms and the enjoyment of executing them with style and panache contributes both to fitness and fittingness.

2-33. Rock-and-roll dancing to the rhythm-and-blues music of black nightclubs quickly spread to the young and the restless throughout the United States. Its fever pitch has been captured perfectly in this painting by Joseph Sheppard (American, born 1930).

The Fabric of Dance: Whalebone and Swirling Silk

by Jean L. Druesedow

3-1. The graceful, formal positions of the dancers in this French scene engraved during the 1770s owed something to the structure and cut of the clothes they wore.

3-2. *Opposite:* This late-seventeenth-century Italian engraving clearly indicates the elaboration of rich ornament typical of gowns worn for grand occasions such as balls.

The measure done, I'll watch her place of stand,
And, touching hers, make blessèd my rude hand.
Did my heart love till now? Forswear it, sight!
For I ne'er saw true beauty till this night.

Romeo and Juliet,
Act I, Scene 2

It is in pursuit of such true beauty—especially that which portends romance—that most costumes for dancing have their genesis. Gala balls have long encouraged dressmakers to lavish as much fantasy and illusion as they can in order to create dresses that achieve the desirable glamour and allure. If the occasion is to be a masquerade ball, then even greater license is given, not just to the participants who can, for a few hours, shed the conventions that rule their lives, but to the dressmakers who are freed from theirs as well. For most of the history of fashion, the ball gown has conveyed the epitome of fashionable femininity and captured the attitudes of society toward the woman and the woman's attitude toward herself and the occasion.

The primary requisite for a dress for dancing is that it move with the dancer and enhance the effect of the music and the dance steps. It is the very structure of the clothes that often controls movement. The eighteenth-century dancers

3-3. *Right:* These late-seventeenth-century shoes are made of white kid embroidered with silk and metal threads.

3-4. *Below:* In contrast to a ball gown, the dress worn at home for a dancing lesson was more modest and had less ornament. The shorter skirt, stylish in the late eighteenth century, was also more convenient for dancing.

3-5. *Opposite:* The elaborate head-to-toe decoration on the costume in this fashion plate of 1779 emphasizes the special nature of the whole toilette appropriate for a grand ball.

depicted in *Le Bal Paré à Monsieur de Villemorien Tila* demonstrate the dance posture of the era. Both men and women hold their backs slightly arched, shoulders back, arms out from their bodies (fig. 1). These postures were the result not only of the dancing master's efforts throughout an eighteenth-century childhood but even more of the corsetry and cut of the clothes. A fully boned eighteenth-century corset allowed a woman to lean backward or from side to side, but she could not bend forward from the waist without the heavily boned point of her corset or its boned shoulder straps reminding her of the correct bearing. The set of the sleeve for both men and women had very little fullness over the sleeve cap at the shoulder, and the sleeves were placed more toward the back of the coat or bodice than we are used to today. Furthermore, the armhole was cut very high and tight. All of this made it much more comfortable to keep shoulders back and arms ever so slightly raised. The shape of the sleeve itself was curved at the elbow rather than straight as we know it, and this also encouraged the wearer to keep the arm in the slightly bent position that we associate with the posture of the eighteenth century.

Throughout most of the eighteenth century, women wore a two-piece dress composed of an open robe worn over an exposed petticoat. All of the women in *Le Bal Paré* are wearing versions of this basic costume. The shape of the skirt varied during the century depending on the structure of the hoops worn to support it. The elliptical side hoops, known as panniers, could be hip length or floor length and could span any number of feet in width. Of course, such panniers affected the ability of the woman to move, the nature of the movement, and the amount of space she occupied in the ballroom. These considerations must have influenced ballroom

Dessiné par Le Clerc   *Gravé par Pelicier*

L'évite de taffetas, ajustée et garnie de gaze autour; ceinture à la mode. La figure est coeffée d'un chapeau
à la Spa. Le maître en peut habit de couleur à la mode, et coeffé en herisson.

A Paris chez Esnauts et Rapilly, rue St Jacques à la Ville de Coutances. Avec Priv. du Roi.

Pl. 66

Dessiné par Le Clere

Gravé par Dupin

Habit de bal avec des manches à la Gabriele et une juppe retroussée en basques seconde juppe à volant garni et mis en guirlande d'une couleur différente de la premiere juppe et uniforme avec les revers des manches et les rubans.

3-6. The French dress *opposite* made of ivory-colored ribbed silk brocaded with serpentine garlands and floral sprays dates to the third quarter of the eighteenth century.

3-7. *Right:* While capturing the whimsicality that so often appears in ball gowns, this French dress from 1802 maintains the fashionable silhouette of the time.

3-8, 9. *Far right and below:* The delicate quality of these two dresses underscores the romantic attitude toward femininity that existed in the early nineteenth century.

arrangements, for when panniers were no longer worn, the commentary in *Galerie des Modes* includes a note of unspoken relief that "the time is past when one finds it necessary to specify on invitations to a ball: *ladies without panniers.* The dancers [now] present themselves in short petticoats and adjusted robes [fig. 4]."

Further examination of *Le Bal Paré* reveals women who wear their petticoats a few inches off the floor with their robes draped at the sides and back so that they are above the hem of the petticoat, a style also depicted in *Galerie des Modes* (fig. 5). At the same time other women in figure 1 seem to wear the older style with their robes flowing into a short train. These women were called "draggers" by the marquise de la Tour du Pin in her memoirs (quoted in Oliver Bernier's *Pleasure and Privilege*).

Shoes such as those in *Le Bal Paré* were made without a right or left, with pointed toes, rounded soles, and high curved heels placed forward almost to the instep, much like the late seventeenth-century shoes pictured (fig. 3). Balancing in such shoes required skill and practice, and executing the intricate footwork of eighteenth-century dances would quickly separate the agile and graceful dancer from all the others.

Movement is also affected by the type of fabric and ornamentation used for the dress.

3-10. *Right:* To complement the romantic ladies, these stylish gentlemen reflect the lasting influence of Beau Brummell.

3-12. *Opposite:* The fashionable silhouette of the 1830s with full sleeves, narrow waist, and wide skirt is evident in both these dresses, as are the typical differences between gowns appropriate for dinner and those for dancing.

3-11. *Below:* This dress of yellow silk gauze trimmed with lace and silk padded piping was made in England in about 1820.

The heavy damasks or crisp silk taffetas of the seventeenth and eighteenth centuries gave an aura of formality to movement. The petticoats themselves were cut only slightly fuller than the circumference of the panniers so that the swirling skirts associated with ball gowns of later centuries were not a factor for an eighteenth-century dress. The ball gown in figure 5 is fairly typical; its

> bodice, with a very low neckline, is ornamented with embroideries or lace outlining the seams. The sleeves are slashed and finished, sabot-style, with lace as on court sleeves, going as far as the elbow.
> The bottom of the robe is covered with a border of trimmings, like those of the bodice and tucked up in drapery...with rosettes and tassels.
> The skirt, different in color from the bodice, is trimmed in Italian gauze worked and shaped like a garland; the bodice, open in front, reveals a short doublet like the skirt whose sleeves are seen through the slashes of the bodice sleeves [*Galerie des Modes,* pl. 66].

The French ball gown in figure 6, which dates from late in the third quarter of the eighteenth century, is trimmed with self-fabric called "robing," edged with multicolored silk fly fringe and rosettes. The elaboration of dresses with all manner of trimmings is one of the distinguishing characteristics of ball gowns generally. In the eighteenth century, Rose Bertin was especially known for creating such trimmings, and her most famous client was the queen, Marie Antoinette.

Except for the more columnar silhouettes of early nineteenth-century gowns, the basic characteristics of the ball gown remained un-

3-13. *Right:* The bell-shaped hoop of the 1850s required evening wraps and coats that were specially constructed to envelop the wearer, as in the case of the taffeta coat at the right.

"The hostess is attentive to the ladies, observing if any timid or unattractive guest receives a noticeably small number of these trifles. With tact she quietly provides her with dances that shall make all favors as nearly equal as is possible upon such occasions of competition."

—Social Etiquette of New York, *1887*

3-14. *Above:* These French dresses by Pingat are examples of the wide, elaborate gowns of the late 1860s. The circumference of the hem of the gown trimmed with black lace is almost twenty feet.

changed. In a "Grecian" tunic shown in *Costume Parisien* in 1802 the bodice is still exaggeratedly décolleté, and, below the Greek-key design that borders the overtunic, a fanciful series of roses sweeps down the skirt to catch the drapery up just below the knee, allowing the slippered feet freedom to dance (fig. 7). By the time the waltz was popular, the Romantic aesthetic had consumed fashion as well as the other arts, and the silhouette was becoming wider at both shoulder and hem. Luckily for the dancers, the skirts

were growing shorter and shoes had become soft, flat slippers.

The two illustrations from *Ackermann's Repository* in 1823 show the figures dancing—at least the artist's interpretation of how these styles moved with the body (figs. 8, 9). Many of the ball gowns of this time were made of very light silks or gauzes with skirts only about seven feet around the hem. Like that of the yellow silk, ribbon-striped gauze dress in figure 11, the hems were often heavily trimmed, here with

large, padded silk piping and white lace. The diaphanous quality of this dress is also an important attribute of many of the fabrics used for dancing dresses throughout the nineteenth and twentieth centuries.

The fashion plate from *Belle Assemblée* (fig. 12) emphasizes the difference between ball dresses and those worn for other evening entertainments, in this case a dinner dress: the ball gown has a more revealing neckline, shorter sleeves, much more varied and elaborate ornamentation; it is, in fact, an exaggeration of the fashionable silhouette and stylish femininity of the 1830s. The coiffure in this plate reflects an attitude that has persisted today: a grand occasion requires special hairdressing. In addition to hair ornaments of intricate and imaginative design, the most spectacular pieces of jewelry in a lady's possession are reserved for full-dress occasions.

By the mid-nineteenth century, the bell-shaped hoop, or cage petticoat, had gained wide popularity and significantly affected the scope and movement of the ball gown. The hoop kept the skirts from entangling the dancer's feet and brought a graceful, swirling motion to the dance. Their size, however, like the panniers of the eighteenth century, required a considerable amount of space in the ballroom and, despite a flexible bone-and-tape structure, mandated space between the dancing partners. In figure 14 the hoops have reached their most exaggerated form, with the circumference of the skirt at its hem nearly twenty feet. Also from this mid-century point, most ball gowns were two pieces: a boned and fitted bodice with a wide, low neckline and short, tight, off-the-shoulder sleeves; and a full, pleated, or gauged skirt worn over the hooped petticoat. Once again the set of the sleeves coupled with the boned bodice and corset insured the proper carriage on the dance floor.

Late in the eighteenth century, Beau Brummell set standards for gentlemen's dress that were widely followed throughout the nineteenth century. A gentleman's full dress consisted, much as it does today, of a very dark blue or black tailcoat and trousers with satin striping on the outseam, white waistcoat, stiff white shirt

3-15. Those present in the elegant ballroom in this painting, *Too Early*, by James Tissot (French, 1836–1902) wear the most stylish gowns of 1873. The abundance of drapery and ruffles mirrors the luxury and elegance of the age.

front, and white tie or cravat. The "top hat, white tie, and tails" of Fred Astaire had its origins in Beau Brummell's fastidious linen and his tasteful rejection of the brocaded silks of the earlier epoch in favor of well-tailored serviceable wool broadcloth. The gentlemen in James Tissot's painting *Too Early* and in James Abbott McNeill Whistler's *Arrangement in Flesh Color and Black* are examples of this familiar style (figs. 15, 16). In European courts, civil uniforms often provided a more gala alternative for gentlemen's dress. In the Viennese court ball in figure 18, the men are in either military or civil uniform.

A number of delightful accessories have been associated with dancing—glass hand-coolers that kept the palms of a lady's hands from revealing the extent of the excitement she endured; dance cards for recording the availability and sequence of partners; bouquet holders of gold or silver suspended from a ring; skirt-lifters, also on a ring, used to manage a train discreetly; fans, so necessary for delicate conversations and recovery from the rigors of the dance.

Over the centuries many of the fabrics chosen for dancing dresses have been light and airy, and so too have the colors, with pale pastels and white predominant through most of the nineteenth century. The dramatic quality of the black gown in John Singer Sargent's *Madame X* (fig. 19) derives in large measure from its color—one that has come to dominate the twentieth century and to represent a high degree of sophistication.

The Belle Epoque, noted for its lavish evening parties and elegant society, expended equal energy on sumptuous evening clothes. The hoops of the 1850s and 1860s became the bustles of the 1870s and 1880s and remained as vestigial pads to round out the hourglass figures of the 1890s. Seen in the paintings by Tissot (see fig.

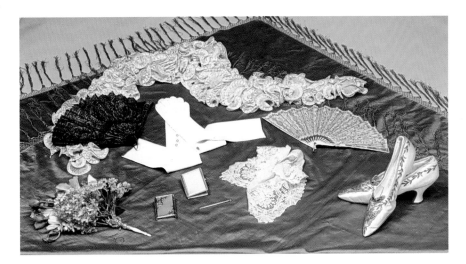

3-17. Among the numerous charming accessories that could be found at the great occasions of the past are those pictured here (from *left*): silk shawl, posy holder, organdy boa, Chantilly lace fan, kid gloves, ivory and silk fan, evening slippers, Brussels lace handkerchief, and two *carnets de bal* by Fabergé.

15) and Gause (fig. 18), the ruffles and ribbons and festooned ornament decorate the ball gowns as exuberantly as social figures decorated their homes.

The arrival in Paris in 1907 of the Ballets Russes crystallized the need for dramatic change in styles and provided a foundation for new attitudes toward design. In fashion this was par-ticularly important in the work of Paul Poiret, who claimed to have freed women from the corset but in fact bound them again, this time at the ankles, with the hobble skirt. The silhouette was remarkably straight by 1915, as demon-strated by the Worth sketch (fig. 23). The sequined net used as an overskirt would float and sparkle as the dancer moved in the new

3-18. *Above:* As seen in *Ball at Court*, a gouache by Wilhelm Gause (German, 1853–1916?), one of the most striking aspects of the dress at a Viennese gala ball was the variety of civil uniforms from the vast reaches of the Austro-Hungarian Empire.

3-19. The elegance of Mme Pierre Gautreau in the famous portrait by John Singer Sargent known as *Madame X* is enhanced by the sophisticated cut and rich black color of her gown. This attitude toward well-cut black dresses has been of great importance in twentieth-century couture.

3-20. *Opposite:* The dresses for a *bal blanc* around 1900 had to represent the youth, innocence, and beauty of the young girl's first venture into society. In this charming watercolor Pierre Vidal uses the swirling skirts of the dancers to capture the rhythm and grace of their movement.

*"To keep her figure she's now obliged to force it
Not to the mould of Canova but a corset."*
*—Robert de Montesquiou,
on Mme Gautreau*

94

dances with Latin rhythms that were gaining popularity. The flat slippers of the early nineteenth century had gradually acquired heels until by the early twentieth century they were over two inches high with a "Louis" curve. They retained at least that height until the 1960s.

In addition to the Ballets Russes, interest in Japan also inspired an exotic orientalism. In an evening-coat design, Mme Paquin captured the kimonolike cocoon shape that allowed luxurious drapery and decoration while maintaining a very narrow silhouette (figs. 21, 22). Evening wraps were created with just as much attention to the special nature of the occasion as were the ball gowns themselves. Often trimmed with rich furs and made of heavy patterned silks, these garments were far more than elegant harbingers of gowns to be revealed when ladies entered the ballroom.

The quintessential flavor of the jazz age is to be found in a 1925 illustration from *Harper's Bazar* (fig. 24). Urbane sophistication reigns in the posture of the dancers as well as in the silhouettes of the dresses but then finds itself juxtaposed with the frivolity of fantastic drapery and ornamentation. Dresses in the twenties permitted the Charleston and black bottom to be danced with abandon because the dresses themselves had abandoned the structure of previous periods. Hanging straight from shoulder to knee, caught only at the hip for emphasis, these dresses had none of the corsetry that inhibited motion. Only the sheer weight of fabric completely covered with glass beads could affect the movement, not to mention the endurance, of the dancer. The vast majority of evening dresses were sleeveless, so arms were freed as well.

By the twenties, brighter colors, which had begun to appear at the end of the nineteenth century and had been given added impetus by the Ballets Russes, found wide acceptance, along with black. Coco Chanel's "little black dress" made itself as indispensable on the dance floor as it was in town for day wear; in the evening version the neckline plunged deeper, the sleeves disappeared, the ornament increased and fluttered more. The dress in figure 26, photographed by Cecil Beaton, is covered with narrow pieces of silk georgette, each sewn with a line of sequins and attached at one end to the dress to create a fringe. Imagine the enhanced effect of the movement with both wearer and sequins dancing. On other dresses, other decorative elements—feathers, beads, silk fringe, floating panels, scarves, scalloped and dagged

3-21, 22. The photograph *opposite* and the plate *above* show the actual Paquin coat in the Costume Institute collection and the illustration published to advertise it in 1912. The spirit of the moment is caught by both the style of the illustration and the dramatic qualities of the costume itself.

3-23. *Left*: It is of special interest to note the fabric swatches attached to this 1915 sketch from the House of Worth. The buyer could choose the color that most suited her when she ordered the dress.

3-24. *Right:* This scene reveals not only the haute couture of Coco Chanel, *left*, and Paquin, *right*, but also the demeanor fashionable in 1925—so different from attitudes of the eighteenth and nineteenth centuries.

3-25. *Left:* The daring of the 1920s is evident in the low neckline and sleeveless style of this short Worth evening dress—evening attire that for the first time bares the lower leg.

3-26. *Opposite:* This flapper dress of 1926, photographed by Cecil Beaton, was the inspiration for a minidress designed in the 1960s by Norman Norell.

3-27. Throughout the 1930s the silhouette was elongated and slender, with the draping qualities of the fabrics enhancing the line, as in these Jean Patou dresses.

hems—all added their own motion to that of the dancer.

The 1930s understood movement in a different way, and the dresses designed by Madeleine Vionnet represent the most imaginative interpretation of this change (fig. 28). Emphasizing the contours of the body itself, these dresses gave the appearance of gliding over the body with no structure at all. Instead, they are consummate examples of a cut so sophisticated that the inherent structure of the textile alone gives shape to the dress. By manipulating the degree to which the bias, or diagonal of the fabric, draped vertically on the body, Vionnet created dresses that moved as one with the wearer. Frequently made of silk crêpe or charmeuse or metallic lamé, these dresses had long sinuous lines of great sensuality. Such fabrics have a reflecting quality, and the play of light and shadow gave added emphasis to the contours of the body in motion.

The exuberance of Christian Dior's "New Look" collection in the spring of 1947 was a return in the cycle of fashion to a silhouette more dependent on shapes imposed on the body by molded bodices, cinched waists, exaggerated hips, and longer skirts. The New Look for evening included some of the most remarkable ball gowns ever created. Strapless bodices brought the neckline lower than ever but required boning that was reminiscent of the corsetry of previous epochs and had a similar effect on the posture of the wearer. Extraordinarily bouffant skirts, such as those in figure 32 and on page 102, brought graceful, swirling movement to the dance floor. Supported by multiple layers of stiff, light crinolines with occasional hoops, these skirts took as much space in the ballroom as their predecessors a century before.

Ball gowns designed by Charles James featured distinctive, structured satin drapery (fig. 33). The outer fabrics of the James dresses were draped over an elaborately constructed shape and, although very heavy, were built in such a way that the weight was balanced, therefore more comfortable for the wearer. The structure of the dresses did control movement, however, through volume as well as boning. Throughout the 1950s, under the fashion leadership of Balenciaga, the silhouette for evening varied from wide to narrow, with an ever more sculptural attitude toward the silhouette. Ball gowns did not always sweep the floor in the fifties; some were cut to ballerina length—just below the calf—or street length—a few inches below the

3-28. *Above:* The drapery of Madeleine Vionnet's bias gowns over a woman's body gave a classical quality to many of her fashions, as is emphasized in this 1931 example, named "Sonia" by the designer.

3-29. *Left:* One of the most influential twentieth-century designers, Coco Chanel, models one of her 1937 creations in her own inimitable style.

3-31. *Left:* This fashion photograph by Man Ray (French, 1890–1976), while featuring a Lucien Lelong dress, reveals the bored sophistication of the late 1930s as well as a taste for shocking juxtapositions.

3-30. *Opposite:* Until the war years brought about sumptuary laws and other shortages, American designers created luxurious evening fashions such as these lace dresses by Milgram and Hattie Carnegie, photographed by Louise Dahl-Wolfe in 1941. The ultrasophistication of the 1930s gave way to a more naive quality in the 1940s.

3-32. *Right:* These dresses, named "Venus" and "Juno" by their designer, Christian Dior, epitomized the return of luxury after World War II.

knee. In the sixties, this trend went even further, encompassing the extremes of the miniskirt and hot pants.

Perhaps no single word better evokes the 1960s than "variety." Dramatic change occurred in popular dance music: rock and roll entered the ballroom, bringing with it the twist and other dances and a range of clothing, from minidresses made of plastic discs by Paco Rabanne to elegant full-length sequined "mermaid" dresses by Norman Norell (fig. 35). Designers created as much variety in structure as in shape. For example, the sequins on the Norell are individually sewn to a fine silk jersey, allowing stretch with the motion of the body, and the Paco Rabanne, linked with metal rings, was flexible at every join. On the other hand, heavily constructed minidresses such as those by Courrèges, with linings and interlinings, left the legs and arms free but maintained rigidly geometric lines.

Accessories in the twentieth-century's middle decades became fewer—gone were hand-coolers, dance cards, bouquet holders, skirt-lifters, and fans. The single most important accessory became the evening bag of metal, mesh, or beaded and jeweled fabric. Evening shoes of fabric matched the dress or were sculpted and jeweled, like the Roger Vivier shoe for Dior on page 8. Evening boots, also often jeweled, were worn with minidresses.

Until the late 1960s, the element of fantasy, ever present in the design of costumes for social dancing, was given its greatest expression in clothes worn especially for masquerade balls. This "fancy dress" apparel, no matter what the century, retained the basic fashionable silhouette of the time and imposed the fantasy on it. For example, in the nineteenth and twentieth centuries, a very popular fantasy was a "Marie Antoinette" or "shepherdess" costume based on

3-33. Heavy satin drapery gives a very sculptural look to these postwar Charles James dresses photographed by Cecil Beaton.

3-34. From the inception of her long career, Mme Grès has used soft silk jersey to achieve gowns of classical grace and sculptural quality, here augmented by the stiffened silk overdress. This 1950 photograph of the model Dovima was made by Richard Avedon.

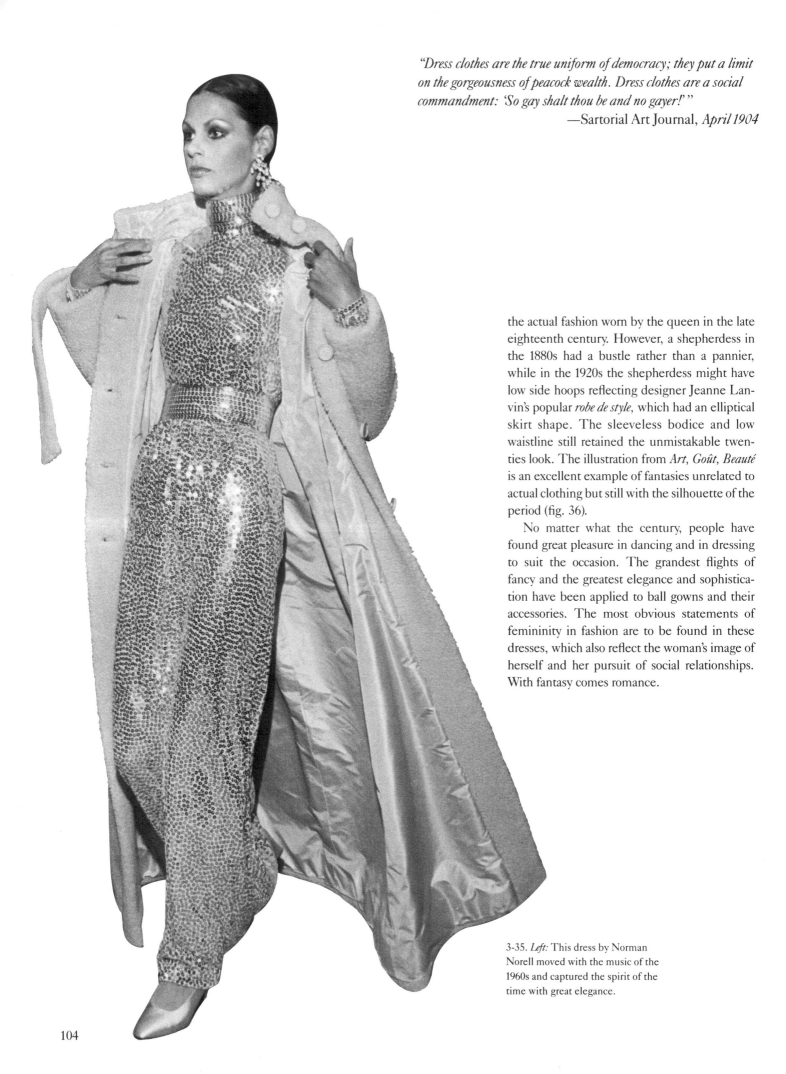

the actual fashion worn by the queen in the late eighteenth century. However, a shepherdess in the 1880s had a bustle rather than a pannier, while in the 1920s the shepherdess might have low side hoops reflecting designer Jeanne Lanvin's popular *robe de style*, which had an elliptical skirt shape. The sleeveless bodice and low waistline still retained the unmistakable twenties look. The illustration from *Art, Goût, Beauté* is an excellent example of fantasies unrelated to actual clothing but still with the silhouette of the period (fig. 36).

No matter what the century, people have found great pleasure in dancing and in dressing to suit the occasion. The grandest flights of fancy and the greatest elegance and sophistication have been applied to ball gowns and their accessories. The most obvious statements of femininity in fashion are to be found in these dresses, which also reflect the woman's image of herself and her pursuit of social relationships. With fantasy comes romance.

3-35. *Left:* This dress by Norman Norell moved with the music of the 1960s and captured the spirit of the time with great elegance.

104

3-36. *Below:* There can be no greater flight of fancy than the creation of costumes for a masquerade ball—all the while retaining fashion, style, and in this case the spirit of the 1920s. These costumes were made to represent seven different stations of the Paris Métro.

"*Crowded tables and a more crowded floor; sleek heads and swaying shoulders; sparkling flash of jewels, real and false; the scent of powders, perfumes, and dust!...College boys and college girls; prosperous men and their prosperous-looking wives; old men and pretty girls; old women and pretty boys; duty dancing, pleasure dancing, bad dancing, good dancing...all this is Florida, in Paris, at one o'clock in the morning.*"

—Vogue, *1 July 1927*

UNE IDÉE ORIGINALE — LES STATIONS DU MÉTROPOLITAIN DE PARIS

3-37. This illustration is from *La Gazette de Bon Ton*, 1921.

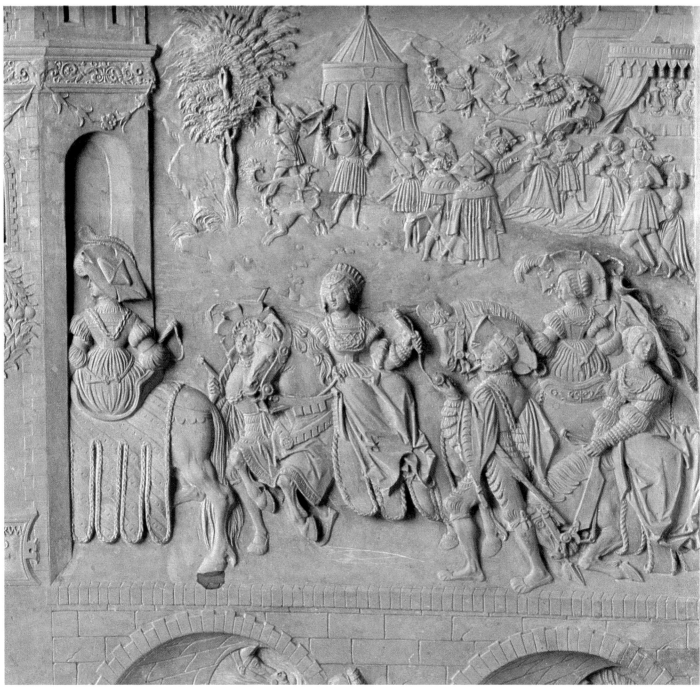

The Iconography of Dance

by Laurence Libin and Constance Old

4-1. *Opposite above:* The carving on the lid of this fifteenth-century Italian marriage chest, or cassone, shows ladies dancing on the occasion of a knight's coronation.

4-2. *Opposite below:* The subject of this sixteenth-century plaque, carved by Johannes Dauer (German, 1485–1538), is an allegory of virtues and vices, but it could be a literal description of a scene at the court of Charles V, where dancing, like hawking, hunting, and jousting, was considered a suitable courtly pastime.

Few activities bring social history more fully to life than old dances; they capture the mood of an earlier age, its music, fashions, and manners. In recent years, growing public appreciation of our cultural heritage has awakened interest in re-creating the dances of days gone by. More than just an amusing pastime, this revival involves both serious scholarship and commercial enterprise. Its concern ranges from the preservation of regional folk dances, some nearly extinct in their native locales, to the re-creation of court ballet, but it centers on reviving urban social dances of the sixteenth through nineteenth centuries. Responding to increasing specialization within the past decade, dance camps and academic workshops have begun to feature instruction in such once-popular dances as Renaissance pavanes and galliards and eighteenth-century gavottes and minuets—the names alone evoke myriad images derived, for many of us, from paintings and book illustrations. Some educators are promoting historical dancing as a participatory activity that offers intriguing insight and experience.

Lavish dance entertainments conceived for aristocratic enjoyment in European palaces are now being staged professionally by rigorously trained Renaissance and Baroque dance companies, which have proliferated hand-in-hand with ensembles of period instruments. Their impressive re-productions, which have recently included grand opera-ballets of Jean-Philippe Rameau (1683–1764), shed new light on the social interactions and brilliant accomplishments of a vanished noble class. Ballroom dances of the nineteenth and early twentieth centuries, closer in spirit to our own time, seem destined for revival as we grow increasingly nostalgic for a more gracious past, made familiar through theater, film, and television. If it is true that interest in a period's music precedes renewal of its dance, the recent rediscovery of ragtime should soon spark enthusiasm for popular dance forms from the turn of the century. Jitterbugging has already come around again, thanks to the reemergence of syncopated swing.

The more academic "authenticity movement" aims to clear away anachronistic misconceptions of how and why early dances were performed and to revitalize beautiful but long-forgotten traditions. In close collaboration, scholars, dancers, and musicians study old treatises, music and dance notations, pictorial and literary descriptions, and antique instruments and costumes in order to understand and express the serious intent of dance masters as distant in time as Domenico da Piacenza, whose treatise *De Arte Saltandi et Choreas Ducendi* dates from around 1416. The social importance of dance in Domenico's time is affirmed by the carving on the lid of a fifteenth-century Italian marriage coffer (fig. 1), which shows ladies dancing to instrumental accompaniment on either side of a knight being crowned; the lid is inscribed *Onessta na belladonna* ("virtue in the beautiful woman"). Like chivalry, dance reinforced medieval gender stereotypes.

Renaissance religious and political leaders as well as pedagogues (among them many Italian Jews, including Rabbi Jacob Levi, son-in-law of the renowned Venetian musician Leon da Modena) considered social dancing a necessary skill, not only because of its role in courtship and entertainment but also because it helped instill accepted codes of behavior. Political as well as moral overtones occur in Johannes Dauer's exquisitely carved plaque, dated 1522, inscribed *Virtutem et viciorum adumbracio* ("a sketch of virtues and vices"), and representing the court of Emperor Charles V (fig. 2). Here, in conjunction with scenes of hawking, hunting, and jousting, four mature couples in courtly garb dance sedately to the music of flute and drum; refreshment awaits them in an open tent. Dance appears in this allegorical context as a symbol of the good life, properly regulated and rewarded.

Much the same message is conveyed by the painted lid of a double virginal by Hans Ruckers the Elder, made in Antwerp in 1581 (fig. 3). This magnificent instrument, which bears the motto *Musica dulce laborum levamen* ("Music, sweet solace of labor") and portrait medallions of Philip II of Spain and his queen, may have been commissioned by the Spanish ruler. With evi-

court of Louis XIV. This monarch, himself an avid dancer, created a royal dance academy at the Louvre in 1661. Two decades later, Ménestrier was able to describe some fifty different ballets in his book *Ballets anciens et modernes selon les règles du théâtre;* by this time theatrical dance had begun to diverge from less demanding amateur court dance. They still shared basic steps, however, and both were often performed to the music of Rameau's illustrious predecessor, Jean-Baptiste Lully (1632–1687), himself a successful dancer and courtier. Lully's *Le Triomphe de l'Amour,* produced the year before Ménestrier's book was published, saw the first

4-3. This beautiful image of a musical party is painted inside the lid of a double virginal made in Antwerp in 1581. Here dancing takes its place among a number of other outdoor summertime activities.

dent approval, the unknown artist places dance in the context of outdoor summertime pleasures—sports and games, boating, feasting, visiting a zoo on the grounds of a château—all, like music, the compensation of aristocratic labor.

The scholar and vicar-general of Langres in eastern France, Jehan Tabourot (better known by his anagram Thoinot Arbeau), whose dance manual *Orchésographie* (1589) takes the form of a didactic dialogue with his imaginary student Capriol ("Caper"), justified dance by citing the Bible: "a time to mourn and a time to dance" (Ecclesiastes 3:4). A continuing esteem for social dance among the ruling class is reflected in the writings of the Jesuit Claude-François Ménestrier, who organized festivities at the

appearance of female professional dancers on the French stage.

The documentary sources through which dance history can be explored are numerous. Early choreographic notation systems, such as the one published by Raoul-Auger Feuillet in his *Chorégraphie* (Paris, 1700), map out hundreds of dances. Scores of informative engravings of dancers appear in books like Gregorio Lambranzi's *Nuova e curiosa scuola de' balli theatrali* (Nuremberg, 1716). Original sketches for dancers' costumes, such as Louis-René Boquet's drawing of Mlle Chevalier "*en grand costume de danse pour le ballet du Roi,*" provide essential details (fig. 4). Chevalier, a mid-eighteenth-century opera singer and actress, was, like others of

4-4. This sketch by Louis-René Boquet (French, 1717–1814) shows the important details of a dancer's dress, in this case the *grand costume de danse* for the ballet of the king worn by Mlle Chevalier, an opera singer, actress, and dancer of the mid-eighteenth century.

4-5. *Below:* This nineteenth-century French fan shows a circle dance among other lively scenes of merrymaking.

4-6. *Right:* The spontaneity of
dance as a purely emotional expression is the subject of this drawing
by Edwin Austin Abbey (American, 1852–1911), who illustrated
Benjamin L. Farjean's novel *A Castle
in Spain.*

4-7. *Below:* Many figures in this
painting by Giovanni Domenico
Tiepolo (Italian, 1727–1804) are
those of actors of the Commedia
dell'Arte, a popular Italian entertainment improvised by stock
characters. The accuracy with
which the clothing is depicted
would enable any contemporary
designer to use it as a model for a
modern masquerade ball.

her profession, a trained dancer. The concealing bulk of her skirt and her stiff bodice, which enforced a perfectly erect posture, imply a concept of grace and motion quite foreign to modern practice; one wonders how she even managed to breathe.

Taking into account the vast number of unexplored sources, the historian Meredith Little has pointed out four fertile areas for future investigation: fifteenth-century Burgundian and Italian court dances; French branles and Italian *balletti* of the late sixteenth and early seventeenth centuries; French court dances from about 1680 to 1725; and popular Baroque dances such as the English country dance and French contredanse, which were performed by all classes of society. To these fairly remote styles we might add more recent ballroom dances of the Romantic era, amply documented in pictures and literature. Certain other dances taught today to children—for example, the familiar, frisky circle dance that figures in scenes of youthful partying on a French nineteenth-century fan (fig. 5)—preserve vestiges of much older adult entertainments. As late as the sixteenth century, elderly aristocrats gravely performed circle dances; eventually, in Western Europe, such dances became the property of young people and the lower classes.

The scholarly and practical activity outlined above, part of a healthy retrospective trend, reacts against the stifling status quo too often imposed by conservatism in the performing arts and entertainment field. The search for inspiration in the past also rises from an urge to place current popular dance fashions in context. Many dancers have adopted a historically informed approach in opposition to the notion that novelty means superiority.

The "newer is better" conceit, which can perhaps be understood in terms of theories of biological evolution but which gives rise to endless fads when applied unthinkingly to the arts, would deprive us of the expressive techniques and interpretive freedom underlying the richly varied styles of earlier dance, styles that formerly delighted sophisticated participants and that still have the power to thrill and move us.

Paradoxically, nothing is fresher or more startling in its originality than something "old-fashioned" revealed in the re-created perspective of its own time. The spark of genius appears in every generation; in dance as in other arts, its communicative power remains undiminished as

long as people remain receptive. Just as accretions of dirt, varnish, and overpainting can be peeled off to reveal masterworks of painting in their true, intended colors, so we can look beyond the accustomed, even comfortable, but often overworked surface of today's typical dance events to restore the vivacity and spontaneity of old-time dance as evidenced in contemporary pictures and reviews.

Folk dance offers perhaps the most refreshing tonic. Edwin Austin Abbey's drawing of a somewhat inebriated couple hoofing it outdoors at a nighttime party (fig. 6) reminds us that dance needs no elaborate preparation or musical accompaniment but arises in purest form as a spiritual expression, an outpouring of the psyche from a depth untouched by fashion and sophistication.

Because the authenticity movement provides challenging alternatives to the usual dance experience without necessarily denying the latter's validity or broad appeal, it has a vitality no less forceful than that of its counterpart the avant-garde, among whom we should include break-dancers alongside Merce Cunningham and Twyla Tharp. Both historicism and futurism yank our sensibilities away from the familiar. Because the quest for historical authenticity can

4-8. *Above:* Although this painting of about 1700 attributed to Jean-Antoine Watteau has been titled *Peasant Dance,* the dancing couple are clearly not rustics. They appear to be performing the same dance as the one shown in Domenico Tiepolo's painting.

never be fully satisfied, it leads in new directions; ever novel, like modern dance, it undermines complacent routine and compels constant reevaluation.

The visual arts offer a wealth of information concerning dance. Choreographers, costume designers, theater and opera directors, and performers are turning increasingly often to art for clues about dancing in different periods and places. Dance iconography, as this study is called, is emerging as a fertile field for research. An artist's vision can help us understand dance by illuminating details of characterization, movement, staging, and style. Domenico Tiepolo's painting *A Dance in the Country* is a case in point (fig. 7). Obviously depicting not a rustic folk dance but a Commedia dell'Arte entertainment on the grounds of a mansion, this painting could serve as a study for a stage set. To the music of winds and strings, a young couple—the man costumed as Mezzetino, the woman perhaps in the character of Columbina—dances alone, attracting only casual interest as other actors and guests converse and mingle. The young woman's dress resembles Mlle Chevalier's, and the man wears flat, soft

dancing shoes. The characteristic mask and headgear also provide perfect models for a designer today, while other items, such as the musical instruments, are much less realistic. The dancers' positions, however, including such details as the man's slightly raised left heel, demonstrate Tiepolo's acute observation of actual dance.

Resembling Tiepolo's dancers though less animated and less richly dressed, the dancing couple in a painting attributed to Watteau are clearly not peasants, despite the picture's modern title, *Peasant Dance*, and bucolic setting (fig. 8). Of significance to the modern choreographer is the close relationship between this couple's positions and the pose of Tiepolo's dancers; they could be doing the same dance, possibly a minuet, caught on canvas in two steps only seconds apart. By collecting and viewing sequentially many such related representations, somewhat in the manner of an animated cartoon, a dance iconographer might tentatively reconstruct entire passages of steps.

Artists captured not only the mechanics of dance but also the cultural attitudes and circumstances that have affected it. No clear class dis-

4-9. *Left:* David Teniers the Younger (Flemish, 1610–90), unlike Watteau, pictures real peasants in his *Peasants Dancing and Feasting,* but only to point a judgmental finger at the raucous behavior of the dancers, who represent the very opposite of proper, aristocratic conduct.

4-10. *Opposite above:* The simple dancers pictured on the side of an eighteenth-century Italian harpsichord may convey a wealth of allegorical overtones if one reads symbolic meaning into the pose of the central dancer and the bagpipes.

4-11. *Opposite below:* Where Teniers was more concerned with characterizing the peasant class than depicting the dance accurately, Raimundo de Madrazo y Garreta (Spanish, 1841–1920), in his 1909 painting *Masquerade Ball at the Ritz Hotel, Paris,* employs a near-photographic realism that allows us to study social behavior and costume as well as a turn-of-the-century form of touch dancing.

tinction appears in dances depicted before the fifteenth century, but in the wake of the peasant revolts of that time, artists became more critical of low-class conduct and began to reveal a differentiation and social hierarchy of dance styles. Court dance held the highest status, followed by civic and peasant dances (the term "folk dance" arose only in the late eighteenth century).

According to the iconographer Walter Salmen, the upper class henceforth claimed decency exclusively for itself and regarded peasant dance as foolish or merely instinctive.

The Flemish painter David Teniers recorded aristocratic condescension in a moralizing painting now called *Peasants Dancing* (fig. 9), which shows activities ranging from assault to public

4-13. *Opposite:* Unlike Schall, Francis Picabia (French, 1878–1953) has produced, in *No. 1 Bird and Turtle,* a dreamlike dance image that seems full of meaning but is difficult to decipher without understanding Picabia's sources.

4-12. Jean-Frédéric Schall (French, 1752–1825), in his portrait of Rosalie Gérard, provides us with an accurate picture of the exquisite costume worn by an eighteenth-century Paris Opéra dancer.

urination. In this unruly scene dance is another symptom of dissipation. Three couples stamp and fling to the raucous skirl of a bagpipe; disheveled and sweating, they lack utterly the grace and decorum of their betters, who inhabit a château in the background. By contrary example, this painting teaches proper conduct; such lascivious dancing is surely disreputable, a mockery of correct, upper-class deportment.

Unfortunately for the historian of choreography, the attitude of Teniers's wealthy patrons colored his vision; it is biased and unrealistic and therefore not reliable as evidence of contemporary dance practice. One of many problems is that no documentation exists from before the nineteenth century to confirm the practice, shown by Teniers, of peasants dancing as separate couples rather than as a single group in a row or ring.

A contrasting though not necessarily objective viewpoint appears in *Masquerade Ball at the Ritz Hotel, Paris* by Raimundo de Madrazo y Garreta (fig. 11). Madrazo seems to update Tiepolo's masquerade with almost photographic accuracy—the painter depicts himself in profile, far right, and his wife, seated at the neighboring table with Emma T. Gary (who bequeathed the picture to the Metropolitan Museum) and her husband. A lavishly bedecked and carefree crowd celebrates their elite status as two couples twirl to the strains of a hidden band; another couple is about to join them after a last sip of wine. A bemused waiter, far left, notices a chair overturned by the exuberant dancers. The foreground couple's close embrace, a normal dance position since the mid-nineteenth century, would have been considered indecent in the original period of their costumes, when waltzing created a scandal.

The lessons taught by such fixed images have broad implications for sociology and anthropolo-

gy. For instance, students of choreometrics (the examination of communication through dance movements), lacking filmed records, must rely partly on artistic representations to support such controversial theses as Alan Lomax's, that dances often reflect and reinforce movement patterns that occur habitually in daily life, as during work and social intercourse. If this relationship between dance and mundane activity is valid, the analysis of dance images may evoke broad impressions of how a society operated in the past.

As we learn from Teniers, the central question of whether or not a particular image faithfully depicts reality is crucial to interpreting dance imagery. Seldom do artists (as opposed to illustrators) content themselves with graphic accuracy in representing people; more often they depart from pure description for aesthetic reasons or to express symbolic messages that may have little to do with the intentions of their depicted subjects. For example, an Italian harpsichord of the early eighteenth century bears on its side a painting of peasants dancing to a bagpipe (fig. 10). Curiously, everyone but the tall woman at center wears a tragic expression; three dancers in a row left of center appear to be blind. This picture does not convey the spirit of a normal folk dance but instead follows the emblematic tradition of *chorea mundi,* the "dance of the world," in which a beautiful woman representing worldly vanity and vice is encircled by dancers seduced by her charms. As in Teniers's painting, the bagpipe can symbolize both a wineskin and a phallus, hence intoxication and lust. Viewed analytically, many seemingly innocent dance images such as this one reveal erotic undertones.

As the previous example shows, one must distinguish meaningful from decorative images and pictures of real dancers, which are rare, from

imaginary visions. Frédéric Schall's revealing portrait of Rosalie Gérard (1752–1820), known as Mlle Duthé, a Paris Opéra dancer and mistress of the duc d'Artois, is a good example of realism in character, pose, and costume (fig. 12). Gérard's midcalf dress style was introduced by Marie Camargo, an earlier dancer at the Opéra, who created a sensation by revealing so much of her legs; henceforth, female dancers had to wear underdrawers. It is not always so easy to identify realism because, confusingly, both dance and art contain inconsistent elements of fantasy, unpredictability, and exoticism. What can be the meaning of Francis Picabia's dreamlike painting *No. 1 Bird and Turtle* (fig. 13)? Picabia, who collaborated with Erik Satie on the Dada ballet *Relâche* (1924), incongruously placed his dancers in a surreal landscape. The dancers' postures are bizarre in their juxtaposition, while the nearly naked woman's spotted body and ecstatic expression—contrasting with her tuxedoed

partner's serious face—and the lightly delineated turtle and bird (which look like afterthoughts) suggest hidden messages. In fact, the animals, landscape, and pigmentation of the woman's body derive directly from old engravings reproduced in a 1925 medical journal to illustrate an article on piebald Negroes.

Somewhat similar in atmosphere, a French seventeenth-century tapestry (fig. 14), indebted to a painting of Apollo and the Muses by Giulio Romano, pictures classically garbed barefoot men and women dancing in an overgrown antique setting. A group of instruments by the stream at lower left (partly rewoven) comprises types associated with rustic revels: tambourine, panpipe, triangle, cymbals, shawm. The vigorous dance is about to break off as the leading youth calls attention to a peacock toward which he runs. The meaning of this apparent allegory is unclear.

Rich in symbolic and emotional content,

4-14. *Left:* Another unclear allegory is this scene on a seventeenth-century French tapestry based on a painting by Giulio Romano.

4-15. *Opposite above:* The photographic sequences of Eadweard Muybridge (American, 1830–1904) made it possible for the viewer to analyze movement more accurately than was possible from any single image.

4-16. *Opposite below:* In this brilliant pencil sketch for his painting *El Jaleo*, John Singer Sargent (American, 1856–1925) is obviously more interested in capturing the impression of a dancer's motion than in depicting accurately her step, costume, or character. However, his spontaneous style expressively conveys the tempo and mood of the dancer.

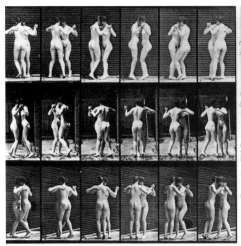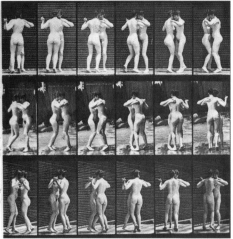

dance, like music, affects people mainly in a nondiscursive manner by arousing feelings and involuntary physical responses. Conveying the dancer's affective, expressive (e)motion through time and space in a static medium requires pictorial solutions that may similarly appear to defy or transcend physical reality. Freezing and analyzing complex body motions, a problem that especially fascinated Leonardo da Vinci, largely eluded art and science until Eadweard Muybridge applied photographic techniques to it (fig. 15); earlier, the sequence and continuity of movements in even so apparently simple an activity as running could be described only partially, with no guarantee of precision. But photographs too can distort what the eye sees, because human vision is informed by expectation and remembrance while film is not. In interpreting dance or indeed any motion, artists rely on visual memory, which is incomplete and selective. Inevitably, even works intended to be fully realistic can only approximate their subject.

When reconstructing a dance step from a picture, one must take into account limitations imposed by restrictive garments and awkward footwear. Instruction books on deportment and theatrical gesture supplement our knowledge of appropriate stances and movement patterns. Other clues come from literature, from choreographic notation, and from music—particularly its articulation, tempo, and rhythm. Finally, though fashions change rapidly, especially in popular dance, traditional steps and patterns span the centuries. The gestures of contemporary folk dances show how apparently similar movements depicted in the past might have been executed.

For most artists, though, even more important than documenting a dancer's motion is creating a vivid impression, a sensation of activ-

4-17. *Right:* Paul Troubetzkoy (Russian, 1866–1933 or 1938) has overcome the weighty nature of his medium by posing his bronze dancer at the point of leaving the ground.

4-18. *Below:* Edgar Degas (French, 1838–1917), unlike Troubetzkoy, was more concerned with revealing a "touch of ugliness" than with idealizing the beauty of his dancer.

ity, as John Singer Sargent has done in a sketch for *El Jaleo* (fig. 16), a painting in the Isabella Stewart Gardner Museum, Boston. Sargent's rapid work aptly conveys the improvisatory style of flamenco, though his model, Marie Renard, was Parisian.

Indicating quick motion ordinarily involves emphasizing such suggestive details as displacement of hair and garments and elevation off the ground. The impression of elevation is particularly difficult to achieve in sculpture, which must somewhere be rooted to a base. Paul Troubetzkoy's nimble *Danseuse* (fig. 17) delightfully overcomes this problem; her extended fingers and toes carry the viewer's eye outward, away from the ground, while the energy of her kick makes us anticipate further motion—we can hardly leave her poised like this, a split second before she leaves the ground. Edgar Degas's study, cast in bronze after his death, is initially less pleasing (fig. 18); his flat-footed model appears to be exercising, not moving in any particular direction. Unlike Troubetzkoy, Degas does not idealize his subject, nor is his concern simply for classic beauty; rather, his dancer expresses what he called a more revealing "touch of ugliness without which, no salvation!"

Knowledge of an artist's intent is not enough to distinguish artistic "truth" from physical reality. We must also assess the artist's ability and reliability. Did he actually witness what he portrays? Was he a participant, with a dancer's grasp of balance and posture? Or is his work guided only by impressions picked up secondhand, in which case it is likely to be bland? Our own kinesthetic experience tells us whether a depicted pose is plausible or incongruous. It is unnatural, for example, to move vigorously and at the same time maintain an impassive face. Pavel Petrovitch Svinjin's *Merrymaking at a Wayside Inn* comes across almost as a caricature, so sedate, nearly bored, are the dancing couples (fig. 19); smoke from the foremost man's cigar rises straight up as though he is standing still, while the fiddler madly saws away and taps his heel. It should be kept in mind that Svinjin, who was in his early twenties when he recorded his impressions of American life while serving as secretary to the Russian consul general in Philadelphia, was merely an amateur artist. The sophisticated painter Fernando Botero, on the other hand, deliberately exploits incongruity in *Dancing in Colombia* (fig. 20). The discrepant scale of Botero's dancers and musicians, and the contrast between the dancers' thrusting energy

4-19. *Left:* Pavel Petrovitch Svinjin (Russian, 1787–1839) was an amateur artist who recorded his impressions of America during a trip made in his early twenties. His fiddler is animated, but the dancers are oddly static.

4-20. *Below:* Fernando Botero (Colombian, born 1932) exploits incongruity in his *Dancing in Colombia* to create a convincing view of a sleazy dance hall.

4-22. *Opposite above:* The figures on this piece of eighteenth-century printed cotton are clearly young sailors dancing "la danse savoyarde," as we can tell from their costume and pose.

4-23. *Opposite below:* The cakewalk is easily identifiable in this wonderfully specific print of about 1907 by George Luks (American, 1867–1933).

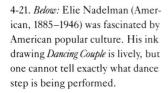

4-21. *Below:* Elie Nadelman (American, 1885–1946) was fascinated by American popular culture. His ink drawing *Dancing Couple* is lively, but one cannot tell exactly what dance step is being performed.

and the bulky band's fatigued stares, are completely unnatural, but the picture convincingly conveys the thick midnight atmosphere of a sleazy dance hall.

Just as a single word from a poem or a chord out of a musical score may not suffice to identify the work (unless it is familiar and unique, like Lewis Carroll's word "jabberwock" or Wagner's *Tristan* chord), so a single image—photograph or artist's representation—of people dancing will usually fail to identify the dance being performed. This is especially likely for popular dances, which hold many postures in common. While a pictured step may be graceful, interesting, and stylistically typical, the arrested motion often lacks enough specificity for a viewer to recognize its context; this is true, for example, of Elie Nadelman's *Dancing Couple* (fig. 21), a product of the Polish-born artist's fascination with American popular culture. Identification is simpler when a dance includes some peculiar pose or prop. A man shown with knees deeply bent, leaning far back as he passes beneath a low bar, can only be doing the West Indian limbo; sailors holding their arms at their sides while leaping to a pipe and drum are most probably dancing a jig or hornpipe (fig. 22); the exaggerated strut of a cakewalk (fig. 23) is hard to mistake. But exceptions like these are rare in conventional social dance.

Unlike traditional dances that involve special equipment (as many sports do) and ballets that tell their story largely through distinctive staging, most popular social dancing at any moment gives few visual indications that would allow someone seeing only a photograph, say, to name the dance with certainty. Such anonymity occurs because popular dancing normally has a limited vocabulary of movements and gestures; in other words, like pop music with its repetitive, usually

4-24. In the early eighteenth century the five basic ballet positions
were first illustrated in *Le Maître à
danser* by Pierre Rameau. Two centuries later ballet, epitomized by
the dancing on *pointe* and the fully
turned out feet seen in Degas's
Rehearsal of the Ballet on the Stage, had
become a highly refined, professionally performed development of
the original aristocratic dance.

4-25. *Left:* This pair of Baroque dancers modeled by Johann Friedrich Lücke (German, active eighteenth century) represents the dancer Mlle Sallé and a male partner wearing a *tonnelet* skirt.

4-26. *Opposite:* The placement of hands on hips and the festive costume indicate that the man depicted in this German bronze sculpture of about 1550 is dancing rather than running.

predictable, chord changes and rhythms, it is highly redundant. Redundancy in dance is both a constraint and a virtue. By having few and simple steps, as a basic box waltz does, popular dance allows full participation even among people with minimal training; partners are free to enjoy one another without having to concentrate on their own motions. It is this deliberate simplicity that keeps a dance down to earth, so to speak, and makes it truly popular.

As dance patterns become more complex and difficult, excluding general participation and eventually requiring professional training, elitism results, and, if the dance is sufficiently enduring and serious in intent, a classical style emerges. We can speak of classicism even in regard to popular dance. Certainly the breathtakingly imaginative, exhilarating, and romantic performances of Fred Astaire and Ginger Rogers lay far beyond the capabilities of average ballroom dancers. These virtuosi raised popular dance to an artistic level that their fans could hardly hope to achieve, just as great jazz improvisers elevated simple chord patterns like the blues progression into a cerebral, elite form.

It is not difficult to see in the five elementary positions of classical ballet a redundancy that recalls ballet's origin as a popular form, albeit an upper-class one. These positions were not nearly so extreme in the Baroque era, when completely turned-out feet and dancing on

pointe, as shown by Degas (fig. 24), were unknown. The five basic ballet positions were first illustrated in *Le Maître à danser* (1725) by Pierre Rameau, French dance master to the queen of Spain. According to the dance historian Wendy Hilton, French *danses à deux* of the seventeenth century were constructed from a basic vocabulary of only about twenty steps, most of which could be incorporated into any dance whether in double or triple meter. The motions making up the step-units were even fewer: walking (*pas marché*), knee bends (*pliés*), rising from the *plié* (*élevé*), small jumps (*sautés*), slides (*glissés*), and turns on the balls of the feet (*tournés*). Each of these motions could be ornamented, and hand and arm gestures were employed along with inflections of the head. These expressive embellishments animate a pair of Baroque dancers (fig. 25) modeled by J. F. Lücke. Performed quickly or slowly in different rhythms, these standardized motions could be combined almost infinitely. At any moment, however, the eye perceives only one pose, and this is the artist's problem.

From the artist's viewpoint of frozen motion, a waltz (derived from the ancient volta) may be hard to distinguish from a fox-trot, or a conga from a bunny hop; they employ much the same body language, and distinguishing motions are seldom visible on the instant. If an artist wants to depict an immediately recognizable dance, he must show a unique, characteristic moment. Often, the more idiosyncratic, athletic, or intricate a dance becomes, the more readily it can be characterized by a single pose—the can-can's high kick, for example, or the Charleston's crossed hands on knees. At the opposite extreme, a very simple dance motion can be indistinguishable from another activity such as running or jumping; thus we may not know from an image whether the subject is dancing at all. Only the placement of hands on hips suggests that a man in festival costume from about 1550 is dancing rather than running (fig. 26).

In all temporally extended arts, a dynamic sequence of events—words, notes, steps—rather than any single unit individualizes the work, carries its plot, so to speak. Thus we refer to "passages" and "pacing" in dance, music, drama, and literature, implying movement onward in time. These terms apply only loosely to static or synchronous arts, and then more properly in regard to creative processes than to elements of the finished work. Only an illusion of rare artistry can save the fixed pose, deprived of its generative force and resolution, from being lifeless. The viewer must be allowed to supply the pose's origin and destination in his imagination by drawing on memory of actual experience. For example, experience tells that a dancer shown in midair must have sprung from the ground near a certain place and will descend somewhere in the direction of forward motion; where we think this will be depends on our impression of velocity. The frozen image thus acts on our remembrance of similar events that we have witnessed or very likely experienced only during childhood play. Without this background, we would fail to respond appropriately, and the dance image would be inexplicable or lacking in intensity.

While no image can fully convey the kinetic feeling of doing or watching a dance, pictures and other immobile, timeless representations can nevertheless reveal much about the nature of dancing and, when identifiable, about particular dances, especially about their style. As portrayed in painting and sculpture, a dancer's costume, position, gesture, facial expression, surroundings, and apparent interaction with other people all contribute visual evidence that is invaluable to the historian and modern interpreter. They also provide the casual viewer with an opportunity for tightly focused attention and sustained contemplation, which live performance seldom affords.

Picture Credits

Frontispiece. Cecil Beaton: *Irene Castle*
Photograph, n.d.
Irene Lewisohn Costume Reference Library
The Metropolitan Museum of Art

Page 8. Richard Avedon: *Evening slipper by Roger Vivier for Dior*
Photograph, 1963
Copyright 1963 by Richard Avedon Inc.
All rights reserved.

1-1. Charles-Nicolas Cochin: *Yew Tree Ball*
Engraving, c. 1745
The Metropolitan Museum of Art. The Elisha Whittelsey Collection, The Elisha Whittelsey Fund, 1930 (30.22)

1-2. "Costume de Paul Poiret dans le goût Louis XIV" from *La Gazette de Bon Ton*, 1912
Thomas J. Watson Library
The Metropolitan Museum of Art

1-3. *Vue perspective de la salle du bal, construite dans la cour de l'Hôtel de Ville*
Engraving, 1750–1760

1-4. Matthew Darly: *A Scotch Reel*
Engraving, 1776
Dance Collection, The New York Public Library

1-5. *The Windsor Ball*
Engraving, c. 1778
Irene Lewisohn Costume Reference Library
The Metropolitan Museum of Art

1-6. Moreau le Jeune: *Le Bal Masqué*
Engraving, 1782
Bibliothèque Nationale, Paris
(Roger-Viollet photo)

1-7. "Domino" from *Galerie des Modes*, 1783
Irene Lewisohn Costume Reference Library
The Metropolitan Museum of Art

1-8. Thomas Rowlandson: *The Comforts of Bath: The Ball*
Pen and ink and watercolor, c. 1798
Yale Center for British Art, Paul Mellon Collection, New Haven, Connecticut

1-9. Social ball invitation, 1813
The New-York Historical Society

1-10. Untitled lithograph, c. 1815
The Bettmann Archive

1-11. *Sketch of a Ball at Almack's*, 1815
BBC Hulton Picture Library, The Bettmann Archive

1-12. *Newport Pagnell. Mrs. Hurst Dancing*, 1816
Copyright Neville Ollerenshaw, 1981
From Diana Sperling: *Mrs. Hurst Dancing and Other Scenes from Regency Life* (London: Victor Gollancz; New York: St. Martin's Press)

1-13. George Cruikshank: *Tom, Jerry and Logic making the most of an Evening at Vauxhall*
Engraving, 1821
Irene Lewisohn Costume Reference Library
The Metropolitan Museum of Art

1-14. "Grand Ball given by the citizens of New York to the Prince of Wales" from *Harper's Weekly*, 1860
The New-York Historical Society

1-15. Jean Béraud: *La Soirée*
Oil on canvas, c. 1880
Musée Carnavalet, Paris
(Art Resource/Giraudon photo)

1-16. Mrs. Cornelius Vanderbilt as "Electric Light," 1883
The New-York Historical Society

1-17. "Vanderbilt Fancy Dress Ball" from *Frank Leslie's Illustrated Weekly*, 1883
The New-York Historical Society

1-18. Pierre-Auguste Renoir: *La Danse à la Ville*
Oil on canvas, 1882–83
Musée d'Orsay, Paris

1-19. Julius L. Stewart: *The Hunt Ball*
Oil on canvas, 1885
The Essex Club, Newark, New Jersey

1-20. Julius L. Stewart: *Key to "The Hunt Ball"*
Watercolor on paper, 1885
The Essex Club, Newark, New Jersey

1-21. Lady Randolph Churchill, c. 1886
Irene Lewisohn Costume Reference Library
The Metropolitan Museum of Art

1-22. "The Centennial Ball in the Metropolitan Opera House" from *Harper's Weekly*, 1889
Irene Lewisohn Costume Reference Library
The Metropolitan Museum of Art

1-23. Paul Nadar: *Costume Ball of the Princesse de Léon*
Photograph, c. 1890
Caisse Nationale des Monuments Historiques et des Sites

1-24. Joseph-Marius Avy: *Bal Blanc*
Oil on canvas, 1903
Musée du Petit Palais, Paris
(Bulloz photo)

1-25. A Boston debutante, 1894
Irene Lewisohn Costume Reference Library
The Metropolitan Museum of Art

1-26. Mrs. Arthur Paget as Cleopatra, 1897
Reproduced by permission of the Chatsworth Settlement Trustees

1-27. Paul Nadar: *Countess Elisabeth Greffuhle in a Worth dress*
Photograph, c. 1900
Caisse Nationale des Monuments Historiques et des Sites

1-28. "Travestis dans le parc" from *La Gazette de Bon Ton*, 1913
Irene Lewisohn Costume Reference Library
The Metropolitan Museum of Art

1-29. J. C. Leyendecker: *Dancing Couple*
Advertisement, 1913
Courtesy of The Arrow Company

1-30. Irene Castle wearing a dancing dress by Lucille, 1914–24
The Metropolitan Museum of Art
Gift of Irene Castle, 1947 (47.57.6)

1-31. "A Dinner-dance" from *Art, Goût, Beauté*, 1929
Irene Lewisohn Costume Reference Library
The Metropolitan Museum of Art

1-32. Cecil Beaton: *Margot Asquith, Lady Oxford*
Photograph, 1927
Courtesy of Sotheby's, London

1-33. Three illustrations from *Eve*, 1922
Irene Lewisohn Costume Reference Library
The Metropolitan Museum of Art

1-34. Howard Thain: *Palais d'Or, New York City*
Oil on canvas, 1928
The New-York Historical Society

1-35. Mrs. Blaine Mallon and Mr. Paul Wrangel, 1931
The Bettmann Archive

1-36. Illustration from *La Gazette de Bon Genre*, 1921
Irene Lewisohn Costume Reference Library
The Metropolitan Museum of Art

1-37. Horst: *Princess Marina, Duchess of Kent*
Photograph, 1934
Courtesy of Horst

1-38. Cecil Beaton: *Loelia Ponsonby, Duchess of Westminster*
Photograph, 1931
Courtesy of Sotheby's, London

1-39. Cecil Beaton: *Wallis Simpson, Duchess of Windsor*
Photograph, 1937
Courtesy of Sotheby's, London

1-40. Debutantes at the New York Debutante Cotillion and Christmas Ball, 1948

Courtesy of The New York Infirmary Beekman Downtown Hospital

1-41. Cecil Beaton: *Daisy Fellowes at the Beistigui Ball* (detail)
Photograph, 1951
Courtesy of Sotheby's, London

1-42. "Valerian Rybar as a Devil at the de Cuevas Ball" from *Point de Vue*, 1953
Collection of Valerian Rybar

1-43. Mona, Countess Bismarck, 1955
Irene Lewisohn Costume Reference Library
The Metropolitan Museum of Art

Page 52 *(counterclockwise from top):*

Martin Engelbrecht: *Das Tanzen*
Engraving, c. 1730
Dance Collection, The New York Public Library

Thomas Rowlandson: *The Comforts of Bath: Private Practices Previous to the Ball*
Engraving, c. 1798
Yale Center for British Art, Paul Mellon Collection

After Emil Adam: *The Dancing Lesson*
Engraving, c. 1880

Jacques-Philippe Lebas: *The Dancing Lesson*
Engraving, late 18th century

Page 53 *(from top):*

George Hunt: *Mr. Owen's Institution, New Lanark*
Aquatint, 1825
Dance Collection, The New York Public Library

George Cruikshank: *The Dancing Lesson*
Etching, 1835
Dance Collection, The New York Public Library

Illustration from *La Gazette de Bon Genre*, 1920
Irene Lewisohn Costume Reference Library
The Metropolitan Museum of Art

Page 54 *(from top):*

Alfred Stevens: *Winter*
Oil on canvas, c. 1875
Sterling and Francine Clark Art Institute, Williamstown, Massachusetts

Louise Dahl-Wolfe: *Dior Ball Gown*
Photography, 1950
Courtesy of Louise Dahl-Wolfe

"Les Préparatifs du Bal" from *Le Bon Genre*, 1801
Irene Lewisohn Costume Reference Library
The Metropolitan Museum of Art

Page 55 *(from top):*

After Paul Gavarni: *Les Apprêts du Bal*
Engraving, 1834
The Metropolitan Museum of Art
Bequest of Howard Carter, 1939 (49.74.141)

Richard Avedon: *Dorian Leigh*
Photograph, 1949
Photograph copyright 1949 by Richard Avedon Inc.
All rights reserved

Page 56 *(from top):*

Hans Lefler: *The Allegory Dance*
Engraving, 1902
The Newark Public Library, Newark, New Jersey

Illustration from *Fashions of London*, 1798
Irene Lewisohn Costume Reference Library
The Metropolitan Museum of Art

Page 57 *(from top):*

Jean-Léon Gérôme: *Duel After the Masquerade*
Oil on canvas, after 1857
Walters Art Gallery, Baltimore, Maryland

Alfred Stevens: *After the Ball*
Oil on canvas, 1874
The Metropolitan Museum of Art
Gift of the Estate of Marie L. Russell, 1946 (46.150.1)

2-1. "Dancers" from *Chronique d'Angleterre*

Miniature painting, 15th century
Osterreichische Nationalbibliothek, Musiksammlung,
Vienna

2-2. Stratonice Master: *Antiochus and Stratonice* (detail)
Panel from a cassone, 15th century
The Huntington Library
San Marino, California

2-3. French School: *Le Bal du Duc de Joyeuse*
Oil on canvas, c. 1581
Musée du Louvre, Paris
(Art Resource/Giraudon photo)

2-4. Unknown artist: *Queen Elizabeth Doing Lavolta with the Earl of Leicester*
Woodcut after a painting in Penshurst Palace, late 16th century

2-5. After Michel-Vincent Brandoin: *The Allemande*
Engraving, c. 1750–80

2-6. "Bal à la Française" from *Almanach Royal pour l'Année MDCLXXXII*, 1685
Bibliothèque Nationale, Paris

2-7. Jean-Antoine Watteau: *Les Plaisirs de Bal*
Oil on canvas, 1717
By permission of the Governors of Dulwich Picture Gallery
(Jeremy Marks photo)

2-8. Beauchamps-Feuillet notation system from *The Art of Dancing a Minuet*, 1735, by Kellom Tomlinson

2-9. Fan, late 18th century
Musée des Arts Decoratifs, Paris

2-10. "La Walse" from *Le Bon Genre*, 1801
Irene Lewisohn Costume Reference Library
The Metropolitan Museum of Art

2-11. "La Trénis, Contredanse" from *Le Bon Genre*, 1805
Irene Lewisohn Costume Reference Library
The Metropolitan Museum of Art

2-12. "La Sauteuse" from *Le Bon Genre*, 1806
Irene Lewisohn Costume Reference Library
The Metropolitan Museum of Art

2-13. *Dottator et Lineator Loquitur*
Engraving, 1817
The Metropolitan Museum of Art
Harris Brisbane Dick Fund, 1942 (42.74.2 [17])

2-14. *L'Eté*
Engraving, 1820–29
Dance Collection, The New York Public Library

2-15. *L'Anglaise*
Engraving, 1820–29
Dance Collection, The New York Public Library

2-16. Viennese dance hall, late 19th century
The Bettmann Archive

2-17. A. Belloquet: "Mabile—La Moment des Confidences" from *Dancing in Paris*, 1860–69
Dance Collection, The New York Public Library

2-18. Paul Gavarni: *La Galope*
Engraving, c. 1830
The Metropolitan Museum of Art, The Elisha Whittelsey Collection, The Elisha Whittelsey Fund, 1952 (52.600.5)

2-19. Schulz: *Bal Valentino*
Engraving, late 19th century
Dance Collection, The New York Public Library

2-20. Feuillet and Desaix choreographic notations, 1713

2-21. Mr. Jullien: *Le Bon Ménage. Contre-Danse Française L'Air et la Figure.*
Engraving, n.d.
The Metropolitan Museum of Art. The Elisha Whittelsey Collection, The Elisha Whittelsey Fund, 1955 (55.563.6)

2-22. "The Basic Step of the Rumba" from *Veloz and Yolanda*, 1945
Irene Lewisohn Costume Reference Library
The Metropolitan Museum of Art

2-23. Pierre Vidal: "Dancing Over the Rooftops of Paris" from *La Vie de Montmartre*, 1899
The Metropolitan Museum of Art, The Elisha Whittelsey Collection, The Elisha Whittelsey Fund, 1954 (54.658.12)

2-24. Henri de Toulouse-Lautrec: *Quadrille at the Moulin Rouge*
Gouache on cardboard, 1892
National Gallery of Art, Washington, Chester Dale Collection

2-25. The turkey trot, c. 1912
The Bettmann Archive

2-26. "Mr. and Mrs. Vernon Castle's New Dances for This Winter" from *The Ladies Home Journal*, 1913
Irene Lewisohn Costume Reference Library
The Metropolitan Museum of Art

2-27. Four girls doing the Charleston in a London stage review, c. 1923
The Bettmann Archive

2-28. Tango del amor, 1927
The Bettmann Archive

2-29. Dance sequence from *Top Hat* (1935)
The Museum of Modern Art, Film Stills Archive

2-30. Lou Barlow: *Jitterbugs*
Wood engraving, 1930s
The Metropolitan Museum of Art, Stewart S. MacDermott Fund, 1983 (1983.1147)

2-31. The twist at the Peppermint Lounge, 1961
The Bettmann Archive

2-32. Jitterbug dancers, 1940s
The Bettmann Archive

2-33. Joseph Sheppard: *Rock and Roll*
Oil on canvas, 1970
Collection of the University of Arizona Museum of Art, Tucson; Gift of the Artist

3-1. A. de Saint-Aubin: *Le Bal Paré*
Engraving, 1770s
The Metropolitan Museum of Art, Harris Brisbane Dick Fund, 1933 (33.56.33)

3-2. *Dama francese in alto di Ballare*
Engraving, 17th century
Irene Lewisohn Costume Reference Library
The Metropolitan Museum of Art

3-3. Shoes
White kid, 17th century
The Metropolitan Museum of Art. Rogers Fund, 1906 (06.1344)

3-4. "The Dancing Lesson" from *Galerie des Modes*, 1780
Irene Lewisohn Costume Reference Library
The Metropolitan Museum of Art

3-5. "Habit de Bal" from *Galerie des Modes*, 1779
Irene Lewisohn Costume Reference Library
The Metropolitan Museum of Art

3-6. Dress
French, c. 1775–1800
The Metropolitan Museum of Art, Purchase, Irene Lewisohn Bequest, 1961 (CI 61.13.lab)
(Sheldan Comfort Collins photo)

3-7. "Tunique de Bal" from *Costume Parisien*, 1802
Irene Lewisohn Costume Reference Library
The Metropolitan Museum of Art

3-8. Ball Dress
Hand-colored engraving, 1823
The Metropolitan Museum of Art, The Elisha Whittelsey Collection, The Elisha Whittelsey Fund, 1942 (42.74.2[29])

3-9. Ball Dress
Hand-colored engraving, 1823
The Metropolitan Museum of Art, The Elisha Whittelsey Collection, The Elisha Whittelsey Fund, 1942 (42.74.2[30])

3-10. Paul Gavarni: *Toilette du Soir*

Lithograph, n.d.
The Metropolitan Museum of Art, The Elisha Whittelsey Collection, The Elisha Whittelsey Fund, 1949 (49.50.339)

3-11. Yellow silk gauze dress
English, c. 1820
The Metropolitan Museum of Art, Purchase, Irene Lewisohn Bequest, 1970 (1970.281.3)
(Sheldan Comfort Collins photo)

3-12. "Dinner Dress and Ball Dress" from *Belle Assemblée*, 1831
Irene Lewisohn Costume Reference Library
The Metropolitan Museum of Art

3-13. Ball Gowns and Evening Coat of the 1850s
The Metropolitan Museum of Art
Summer evening gown, Gift of Mrs. John L. Proctor, 1942 (CI 42.39.2)
Evening dress, Gift of Russel Hunter, 1959 (CI 59.35.2)
Evening coat, Gift of Estate of Mrs. Robert B. Noyes, 1943 (CI 43.7.8)
(Sheldan Comfort Collins photo)

3-14. Ball Gowns by E. Pignat and Cie
French, 19th century
The Metropolitan Museum of Art, Gift of Mary Pierrepont Beckwith, 1969 (CI 69.33 lab and CI 69.33.12ab)
(Taishi Hirokawa photo)

3-15. James Tissot: *Too Early*
Oil on canvas, 1873
Guildhall Art Gallery
(Bridgeman Art Library photo)

3-16. James Abbott McNeill Whistler: *Arrangement in Flesh Color and Black*
Oil on canvas, c. 1883
The Metropolitan Museum of Art, Wolfe Fund, Catharine Lorillard Wolfe Collection, 1913 (13.20)

3-17. Accessories of the ball (from left):
Shawl of changeant silk: The Metropolitan Museum of Art, Gift of Mrs. William H. Johns, 1944 (CI 44.92.6)
Posy holder of gilt and mother-of-pearl: Collection of Carolyn Solomon
Boa of pleated silk organdy: The Metropolitan Museum of Art, Gift of Mrs. Earl Rowe, 1951 (CI 51.15.6)
Lace fan: The Metropolitan Museum of Art, Gift of Mrs. W. Whitewright Watson, 1939 (CI 39.127, 4ab)
Kid gloves with pearl buttons: The Metropolitan Museum of Art (unaccessioned)
Ivory fan with silk and sequins: The Metropolitan Museum of Art, Gift of Agnes Miles Carpenter, 1955 (CI 55.43.23)
Evening slippers: The Metropolitan Museum of Art, Gift of Julia B. Henry, 1978 (1978.288.54ab)
Lace handkerchief: The Metropolitan Museum of Art, Gift of Adele Simpson, 1954 (CI 54.45.7)
Fabergé carnets de bal: Courtesy of A la Vieille Russie, New York
Flowers: Courtesy of Shepard-Clark

3-18. Wilhelm Gause: *Ball at Court*
Gouache on paper, 1900
Museen der Stadt, Vienna
(Lynton Gardiner photo)

3-19. John Singer Sargent: *Madame X*
Oil on canvas, 1884
The Metropolitan Museum of Art, Arthur Hoppock Hearn Fund, 1916 (16.53)

3-20. Pierre Vidal: *Washington Palace, Boston Blanc*
Watercolor, black ink, and wash over pencil, 1908
The Metropolitan Museum of Art, The Elisha Whittelsey Collection, The Elisha Whittelsey Fund, 1950 (50.606[31])

3-21. Evening wrap by Paquin, 1912
The Metropolitan Museum of Art, Gift of Mrs. Edwin Stewart Wheeler, 1956 (CI 56.2.1)
(Sheldan Comfort Collins photo)

3-22. Evening wrap by Paquin from *La Gazette de Bon Ton*, 1912
Thomas J. Watson Library
The Metropolitan Museum of Art

3-23. Jean Worth: Fashion sketch, c. 1915
Irene Lewisohn Costume Reference Library
The Metropolitan Museum of Art

3-24. Dance dresses from *Harper's Bazar*, 1925
Irene Lewisohn Costume Reference Library
The Metropolitan Museum of Art

3-25. "La Douce Nuit" (dance dress by Worth) from *La Gazette de Bon Ton*, 1920
Irene Lewisohn Costume Reference Library
The Metropolitan Museum of Art

3-26. Flapper dance dress, 1926
The Metropolitan Museum of Art, Gift of Mrs. Adam Gimbel, 1942 (CI 42.33.3)
(Cecil Beaton photo)

3-27. Dresses by Patou, 1933
Cooper Hewitt Picture Library

3-28. "Sonia" (gown) by Vionnet, 1931
F. C. Gundlach Collection, Hamburg
(George Hoyningen-Huene photo)

3-29. Cecil Beaton: *Coco Chanel*
Photograph, 1937
Courtesy of Sotheby's, London

3-30. Louise Dahl-Wolfe: *Dresses by Milgram and Hattie Carnegie*
Photograph, 1941
Irene Lewisohn Costume Reference Library
The Metropolitan Museum of Art

3-31. Man Ray: *Lucien Lelong Dress*
Photograph, 1937
Courtesy of Timothy Baum, New York

3-32. Dresses by Christian Dior, 1949
Evening dress of silk tulle: The Metropolitan Museum of Art, Gift of Mrs. Byron C. Foy, 1953 (CI 53.40.7a-e)
Evening dress of tulle: The Metropolitan Museum of Art, Gift of Mrs. Byron C. Foy, 1953 (CI 53.40.5a-e)
(Sheldan Comfert Collins photo)

3-33. Cecil Beaton: *Dresses by Charles James*
Photograph, 1948
Courtesy of Sotheby's, London

3-34. Richard Avedon: *Dovima*
Photograph, 1950
Copyright 1950 by Richard Avedon Inc.
All rights reserved

3-35. Bill Cunningham: *Norman Norell Dress*
Photograph, 1972
Courtesy of Bill Cunningham

3-36. "Travesties" from *Art, Goût, Beauté*, 1927
Irene Lewisohn Costume Reference Library
The Metropolitan Museum of Art

3-37. "Musique de ce temps" from *La Gazette de Bon Ton*, 1921
Irene Lewisohn Costume Reference Library
The Metropolitan Museum of Art

4-1. Walnut cassone
Italian, 15th century
The Metropolitan Museum of Art, Gift of George Blumenthal, 1941 (41.100.188)

4-2. Johannes Dauer: *Allegory of Virtues and Vices at the Court of Charles V* (detail)
Carved honestone plaque, 1522
The Metropolitan Museum of Art, Gift of J. Pierpont Morgan, 1917 (17.190.745)

4-3. Hans Ruckers the Elder: *Musical Party* (detail)
Lid painting on double virginal, 1581
The Metropolitan Museum of Art, Gift of B. H. Homan, 1929 (29.90)
(Schecter Lee photo)

4-4. Louis-René Boquet: *Mlle Chevallier en grand costume de danse pour le ballet du Roi*
Black chalk and watercolor on paper, c. 1745

The Metropolitan Museum of Art, Gift of Mr. and Mrs. Charles Wrightsman, 1966 (66.91)

4-5. Decorated fan
French, mid-19th century
The Metropolitan Museum of Art, Gift of Mrs. William Randolph Hearst, 1963 (63.90.131)

4-6. Edwin Austin Abbey: *The Dance*
Pen and ink on paper, c. 1890
The Metropolitan Museum of Art, Rogers Fund, 1921 (21.103)

4-7. Giovanni Domenico Tiepolo: *A Dance in the Country*
Oil on canvas, c. 1750
The Metropolitan Museum of Art, Gift of Mr. and Mrs. Charles Wrightsman, 1980 (1980.67)

4-8. Attrib. to Jean-Antoine Watteau: *Peasant Dance*
Oil on wood, c. 1700
The Metropolitan Museum of Art, Bequest of Lillian S. Timken, 1959 (60.71.20)

4-9. David Teniers the Younger: *Peasants Dancing and Feasting*
Oil on canvas, mid-17th century
The Metropolitan Museum of Art, Purchase, 1871 (71.99)

4-10. Unknown artist: *Folk Dance*
Harpsichord case, c. 1725
The Metropolitan Museum of Art, Gift of Bernice Richard, 1980 (1980.146)

4-11. Raimundo de Madrazo y Garreta: *Masquerade Ball at the Ritz Hotel, Paris*
Oil on canvas, 1909
The Metropolitan Museum of Art, Bequest of Emma T. Gary, 1934 (37.20.3)

4-12. Jean-Frédéric Schall: *Mlle Duthé*
Oil on wood, c. 1775
The Metropolitan Museum of Art, Gift of Mrs. William M. Haupt, from the collection of Mrs. James B. Haggin, 1965 (65.242.8)

4-13. Francis Picabia: *No. 1 Bird and Turtle*
Gouache on paper, c. 1925
The Metropolitan Museum of Art, Alfred Stieglitz Collection, 1949 (49.70.16)

4-14. *Dance of Shepherds and Shepherdesses*
Tapestry, 17th century
The Metropolitan Museum of Art, Gift of Julia A. Berwind, 1953 (53.225.11)

4-15. Eadweard Muybridge: "Nude Women Dancing" from *Animal Locomotion*, 1887

4-16. John Singer Sargent: *Study for El Jaleo*
Pencil and wash on paper, c. 1882
The Metropolitan Museum of Art, Gift of Mrs. Francis Ormond, 1950 (50.130.139)

4-17. Paul Troubetzkoy: *Danseuse*
Bronze, 1914
The Metropolitan Museum of Art, Rogers Fund, 1929 (29.137)

4-18. Edgar Degas: *Fourth Position Front, on the Left Leg*
Bronze, 1882–95
The Metropolitan Museum of Art, Bequest of Mrs. H. O. Havemeyer 1929, H. O. Havemeyer Collection (29.100.394)

4-19. Pavel Petrovitch Svinjin: *Merrymaking at a Wayside Inn*
Watercolor on paper, 1942
The Metropolitan Museum of Art, Rogers Fund, 1942 (42.95.12)

4-20. Fernando Botero: *Dancing in Colombia*
Oil on canvas, 1980
The Metropolitan Museum of Art, Anonymous Gift, 1983 (1983.251)

4-21. Elie Nadelman: *Dancing Couple*
Ink and wash on paper, c. 1917–19
The Metropolitan Museum of Art, Gift of Lincoln Kirstein, 1965 (65.12.11)

4-22. Lecler père et fils: *Young Sailors Dancing* (detail)
Printed cotton panel, c. 1780
The Metropolitan Museum of Art, Gift of Mrs. W. D. Frishmuth, 1913 (13.166.1)

4-23. George Luks: *Cakewalk*
Monotype in black ink on paper, c. 1907
The Delaware Art Museum, Wilmington, Gift of Helen Farr Sloan

4-24. Edgar Degas: *Rehearsal of the Ballet on the Stage*
Oil and watercolor over ink on paper, c. 1874
The Metropolitan Museum of Art, Bequest of Mrs. H. O. Havemeyer, 1929, H. O. Havemeyer Collection (29.160.26)

4-25. Johann Friedrich Lücke: *Minuet Dancers*
Hard-paste porcelain, 1758
The Metropolitan Museum of Art, Gift of Irwin Untermyer, 1964 (64.101.286, 287)

4-26. Unknown artist: *Man in Festival Costume*
Bronze, c. 1550
The Metropolitan Museum of Art, Gift of Irwin Untermyer, 1964 (64.101.1551)